Blackballed By History

True Tales of Some of History's Most Demonized Characters

Compiled by Paul T. Angel

American Free Press 2014

Table of Contents

Introduction: History Is a Strange Thing 3
Henry Ford on Benedict Arnold 7
Benedict Arnold's Letter to America 23
Banastre Tarleton 27
William Quantrill 29
John Wesley Hardin 45
Waffen-SS General Leon Degrelle on Adolf Hitler 53
Who Was Leon Degrelle? 58
Willis A. Carto on John Amery 75

Blackballed by History:

True Tales of Some of History's Most Demonized Characters

ISBN: 978-0-9881997-5-0

ORDERING: ***Blackballed by History*** (softcover, 77 pages, $15 plus $4 S&H inside the U.S.) can be ordered from AFP, 645 Pennsylvania Avenue SE, #100, Washington, D.C. 20003. To charge by phone call 1-888-699-NEWS toll free and use Visa, MasterCard, AmEx or Discover. See more books and videos from American Free Press at www.AmericanFreePress.net.

American Free Press, 645 Pennsylvania Avenue SE #100, Washington, D.C. 20003
Toll Free Ordering: 1-888-699-NEWS • website: www.AmericanFreePress.net

Foreword: History Is a Strange Thing

History is a strange thing—when you read it, you never can be quite sure what to believe—who is a "good guy" and who is a "bad guy," for example. Some people are purely evil—such as Lenin or Trotsky. Some are all good—Saint Francis of Assisi comes to mind. But most folks are a mixture of good and evil. In this book we take a look at some of history's most celebrated "bad boys," and some who have been forgotten, and find they may not be quite as black as they have been painted. Establishment historians—the court historians, as we in the authentic history movement call them—have a way of twisting things, like your daily paper and the talking air heads on TV do. The smear machine keeps grinding out libel after libel, lie after lie.

We'll even reconsider Adolf Hitler, supposedly the worst bad guy of all time. That chapter is by Leon Degrelle, who himself has been subjected to blackballing by the establishment, but who really is a hero, and, as an eyewitness to history, knew Mr. Hitler personally. Degrelle's writings have been banned in many European countries—usually a good sign that someone is writing the truth.

In this slim volume we obviously cannot hope to rewrite all of history to conform to the facts, much as it needs to be done, but we can aim to give you, dear reader, some significant truths to chew on.

We'll look at, besides Hitler, such boogeymen as Benedict Arnold, a man whose name has become synonymous with "traitor." This chapter is by no lesser a light than the famous Henry Ford, the man behind the Model T car. Most people have forgotten that Arnold started out as a great patriot-hero, without whom the American War for Secession from the British Empire could not have been won. It was only when he fell in with several rotten apples that he turned his coat: British sympathizers, even a British officer, and Jewish war profiteer David Franks. Ironically, when Arnold was still a patriot, he was wounded in battle due to the actions of an earlier traitor, Gen. James Wilkinson. Even after turning his coat, Arnold criticized "the class of men who are criminally protracting the war," as you can see in his letter to the American people, also reproduced in this volume.

And what about "Bloody" Banastre Tarleton? Well known to students of the American Revolution, he is virtually a cipher to the man in the street. But Tarleton achieved notoriety in his time when his men bayoneted wounded American patriot soldiers where they lay. Could there be anything good about this monster?

We Americans, author Paul Angel points out, dislike to remember the Pyle Massacre. In that horrid 1781 event, patriot militia leader Col. Henry Lee fooled hapless loyalist militiamen under Col. John Pyle into thinking he was none other than Tarleton himself, come to join forces with them. In the ensuing battle, 93 loyalists were slaughtered. The unfair nature of the event is reflected in the fact that the patriot losses amounted to one dead horse.

In the 1780 Waxhaw Massacre, which gets more ink in America than the Pyle defeat, Tarleton may have been incapacitated at the time of the atrocity.

Tarleton surely got bad press from the Americans, who needed a boogeyman to hate. Some of the stories circulated about him cannot be verified and may be fabricated. Therefore he may not be nearly as evil as he has been depicted.

Our next author, Clint Lacy, an expert on the American un-Civil War, treats us to an authentic history of William Quantrill—the notorious Confederate guerrilla fighter in the War for Southern Independence. Mainstream historians say he was a ruthless, psychopathic killer. But the facts show he and his men were patriots, fighting for their homes and families. James Lane, who you probably never heard of, committed acts far more destructive before Quantrill's historic Lawrence raid—and Lane was on the Union side. Yet we never hear about Lane. This illustrates the dictum that history is (mostly) written by the victorious—who give it their own slant.

Another "bad boy" you might not have heard of—John Wesley Hardin—was perhaps the greatest gunfighter of the Old West. Author Gary Yarbrough, in this chapter of fascinating Americana, argues that Hardin was a refugee of sorts—a refugee from injustice. Like Robin Hood, that is the reason he lived the outlaw life and, like Robin Hood, he was a folk icon. But Hardin, politically incorrect, has been relegated to the memory hole by the court historians.

Next is the chief devil himself, Adolf Hitler—possibly one of the most virtuous men to live in the past thousand years or two. But rather than trying to correct the historical record on Hitler, which would take thousands of pages, we instead offer Gen. Leon Degrelle's speculation about what would have happened had Hitler won the war, as several time he nearly did? That is the question of alternative history Leon Degrelle ponders in his chapter. What would our world today be like? You might be surprised at his conclusions.

Lastly Willis Carto, founder and publisher of THE BARNES REVIEW, the journal of Revisionist history and nationalist thought, tackles the question of controversial Briton John Amery. Was Amery a traitor, as the court historians insist, or was he an unsung hero of Britain? Carto lays out the facts of the case for you to decide.

As you can see, we have prepared a rich repast of food for the mind in these humble pages, and we know you'll enjoy the read.

—JOHN TIFFANY
Assistant Editor
THE BARNES REVIEW

Benedict Arnold

HENRY FORD ON BENEDICT ARNOLD

BENEDICT ARNOLD WAS A HERO . . . AND THEN A TRAITOR. The worst kind of traitor. One who would turn his back on his nation and his best friend. One who would turn on his own in battle, capturing and burning Richmond, Va. at the head of British troops after his defection. But Arnold's real problem with Congress and his superiors in the military began when a number of bad acquaintances converged in Arnold's life. This included British Major John André, loyalist-leaning Peggy Shippen and David Solesbury Franks, a Jewish specialist in profiting from military contracts. Originally written and published by Henry Ford in his *Dearborn Independent* in 1921, the article avoids the political correctness so prevalent today.

BY HENRY FORD

The part taken by Jews in the wars of the United States has been a subject of considerable boasting by Jewish publicists. It is a most interesting subject. It deserves the fullest possible treatment. It is not *The Dearborn Independent*'s present purpose to challenge the Jewish boast; it is, however, our purpose to fill in the omitted parts of the story, and supply the missing links in several of the most interesting episodes in American history. This will be done on the basis of unquestioned historical authority, mostly of a Jewish character, and solely in the interests of a complete understanding of a matter which Jewish leaders have brought to the front. The first subject that will be treated in this [*Dearborn Independent*] series is the part of Jews in the treason of Benedict Arnold.

MOST CONSPICUOUS TRAITOR

Arnold, the most conspicuous traitor in American history, has been the subject of considerable comment of late. Among the commentators have been

American Jews who have failed to make known to the American public the information which may be found in Jewish archives concerning Arnold and his associates.

To begin with, the propensity of Jewish folks to engage in the business of supplying the needs of armies and to avail themselves as far as possible of war contracts, is of long standing and notice.

An authority on this matter, Werner Sombart, says in his *Jews and Modern Capitalism* (50-3):

> The Jews throughout the 16th, 17th and 18th centuries were most influential as army purveyors and as the moneyed men to whom the princes looked for financial backing. . . . [W]e cannot attempt to mention every possible example. We can only point the way; it will be for subsequent research to follow.
>
> Although there are numerous cases on record of Jews acting in the capacity of army contractors in Spain previous to 1492, I shall not refer to this period, because it lies outside the scope of our present considerations. We shall confine ourselves to the centuries that followed, and begin with England.
>
> In the 17th and 18th centuries the Jews had already achieved renown as army-purveyors. Under the Commonwealth the most famous army contractor was Antonio Fernandez Carvajal, "the great Jew," who came to London some time between 1630 and 1635, and was very soon accounted among the most prominent traders in the land. In 1649 he was one of the five London merchants entrusted by the council of state with the army contract for corn. It is said that he annually imported into England silver to the value of £100,000. In the period that ensued, especially in the wars of William III, Sir Solomon Medina was "the great contractor," and for his services he was knighted, being the first professing Jew to receive that honor.
>
> It was the same in the wars of the Spanish Succession; here, too, Jews were the principal army contractors. In 1716 the Jews of Strasburg recall the services they rendered the armies of Louis XIV by furnishing information and supplying provisions. Indeed, Louis XIV's army contractor-in-chief was a Jew, Jacob Worms by name; and in the 18th century Jews gradually took a more and more prominent part in this work. In 1727 the Jews of Metz brought into the city in the space of six weeks, 2,000 horses

for food and more than 5,000 for remounts. Field Marshal Maurice, of Saxony, the victor of Fontenoy, expressed the opinion that his armies were never better served with supplies than when the Jews were contractors. One of the best known of the army contractors in the time of the last two Louises was Cerf Beer, in whose patent of naturalization it is recorded that ". . . in the wars which raged in Alsace in 1770 and 1771 he found the opportunity of proving his zeal in our service and in that of the state."

Similarly the house of Gradis, of Bordeaux, was an establishment of international repute in the 18th century. Abraham Gradis set up large storehouses in Quebec to supply the needs of the French troops there. Under the Revolutionary Government, under the Directory, in the Napoleonic wars it was always the Jews who acted as purveyors. In this connection a public notice displayed in the streets of Paris is significant. There was a famine in the city and the Jews were called upon to show their gratitude for the rights bestowed upon them by the Revolution by bringing in corn. "They alone," says the author of this notice, "can successfully accomplish this enterprise, thanks to their business relations, of which their fellow citizens ought to have full benefit." A parallel story comes from Dresden. In 1720 the court Jew, Jonas Meyer, saved the town from starvation by supplying it with large quantities of corn. (The chronicler mentions 40,000 bushels.)

All over Germany, the Jews from an early date were found in the ranks of the army contractors. Let us enumerate a few of them. There was Isaac Meyer in the 16th century, who, when admitted by Cardinal Albrecht as a resident of Halberstadt in 1537, was enjoined by him, in view of the dangerous times, "to supply our monastery with good weapons and armor." There was Joselman von Rosheim, who in 1548 received an imperial letter of protection because he had supplied both money and provisions for the army. In 1546 there is a record of Bohemian Jews who provided greatcoats and blankets for the army. In the next century another Bohemian Jew, Lazarus by name, received an official declaration that he "obtained either in person or at his own expense, valuable information for the imperial troops, and that he made it his business to see that the army had a good supply of ammunition and clothing." The great elector also had recourse to Jews for his military needs. Leimann Gompertz and Solomon Elias were his contractors for cannon, powder and so forth.

Arnold & Montgomery Betrayed at the Battle of Quebec

The ill-fated Battle of Quebec was an attempt, on Dec. 31, 1775, by American colonial forces to capture the city of Quebec and enlist French Canadian support for the American Revolutionary War. The British commander, Gen. Guy Carleton, was hemmed in and could not get troops and supplies via the frozen St. Lawrence River. He instead relied on a small number of regulars along with local militia that had been raised in the city. Gen. Richard Montgomery and Col. Benedict Arnold led a force of about 1,000 American forces in a multi-pronged attack on the city which, due to bad weather and bad timing, ended with Montgomery dead, Arnold wounded, and Daniel Morgan and over 400 others captured. **Above**, Continental troops are led into an ambush at the northern barricades of the lower town. Expecting little resistance in this part of the city, the Americans were suddenly fired upon from the windows and doorways of the homes lining the streets. Ironically, as it would turn out, one of Montgomery's own men—a Rhode Island sergeant—had turned traitor and warned the British of the American attack plan. Arnold was wounded in the ankle trying to take a fortified barricade.

> There were numerous others: Samuel Julius, remount contractor under the Elector Frederick Augustus of Saxony; the Model family, court purveyors and army contractors in the duchy of Aensbach in the 17th and 18th centuries are well known in history. In short, as one writer of the time pithily expresses it, "all the contractors are Jews, and all the Jews are contractors." Austria does not differ in this respect from Germany, France and England. The wealthy Jews who in the reign of the Emperor Leopold received permission to resettle in Vienna (1670)—the Oppenheimers, Wertheimers, Mayer Herschel and the rest— were all army contractors. And we find the same thing in all the countries under the Austrian crown.
>
> Lastly, we must mention the Jewish army contractors who provisioned the American troops in the Revolutionary and Civil wars.

Sombart's record ceases there. He does not go on to mention "the Jewish contractors who provisioned the American troops in the Revolutionary and Civil wars." That task shall be *The Dearborn Independent*'s from time to time in the future.

MONEYMAKING OUT OF WAR

It is in the study of Jewish moneymaking out of war that the clues are found to most of the great abuses of which Jews have been guilty. In the present instance, it was in the matter of profiteering in war goods, that the Jewish connections of Benedict Arnold were discovered.

"Wars are the Jews' harvests" is an ancient saying. Their predilection for the quartermaster's department has been observed anciently and modernly. Their interest being mostly in profits and not in national issues; their traditional loyalty being to the Jewish nation, rather than to any other nation; it is only natural that they should be found to be the merchants of goods and information in times of war—that is, the war profiteers and the spies. As the unbroken program is traced through the Revolutionary War, through the American Civil War, and through the Great War of recent occurrence [World War I—Ed.], the only change observable is the increasing power and profit of the Jews.

Although the number of Jews resident in the American colonies was very small, there were enough to make a mark on the Revolutionary War; and while there was no wholesale legislation against Jews as there was in the Civil War, there were actions against individuals for the same causes which in 1861-65 obtained more extensively.

The Journals of the Continental Congress contain numerous entries of payments made to Jews, as well as the records of various dealings with them on other scores. For drums, for blankets, for rifles, for provisions, for clothing—these are the usual entries. Most of the Jewish commissars were Indian traders (the extent to which the Jews dealt with the American Indians has not as yet been made a subject of research it deserves). The Gratz family of Pennsylvania carried on a very extensive Indian trade and amassed a vast fortune out of it. A most curious lot of information concerning the dealings of the Colonies with the Jews is obtainable by a search through old records.

The Jews of Colonial New York were both "loyalists" and "rebels," as the tide turned. They profited under loyalism by the contracts which they secured, and by buying in the confiscated property of those who were loyal to the American cause. It is interesting to note that some of the purchasers of the extensive De Lancey properties were Jews. [James] De Lancey [1703-60—Ed.] was a patriot whom New York City afterward honored by giving his name to an important thoroughfare. That same New York has recently by official action separated the name of De Lancey from that thoroughfare and substituted the name of Jacob H. Schiff, a Jew, native of Frankfort-on-the-Main.

MEET THE FRANKS

We enter immediately into the limits of the Benedict Arnold narrative by making mention of the Franks family of Philadelphia, of which family several members will claim our attention.

A Jewish family from England who settled in America, the Franks retained their English connections. They were in the business of public contracts, principally army contracts. They were holders of the British army contracts for the French and Indian wars, and for the succeeding Revolutionary War.

To get the picture, conceive it thus, as it is taken from Jewish sources:

• Moses Franks lived in England, doing business with the British government directly. He had the contract for supplying all the British forces in America before military trouble between the Colonies and the "home government" was thought of. He was the principal purveyor of the British army in Quebec, Montreal, Massachusetts, New York and in the country of the Illinois Indians. It was all "British territory" then.

• Jacob Franks lived in New York. He was American representative of Moses Franks of England. He was the American agent of the Franks Army

The Workhorse of the Military . . .

In the American Revolution, the *bateau*—a thin, long, light low-draft riverboat that could be manually hauled over land or maneuvered down tricky waterways with poles—was called the "workhorse" of the military. In 1775, it was used to carry supplies for Benedict Arnold's march to Quebec, made through dense forest, swamp and bog. At every spot where a waterway got too shallow, Arnold's men simply picked up the boats and began carrying them. Washington and Rochambeau used *bateaux* extensively to move troops and supplies on the Hudson River and at Yorktown.

Purveyors Syndicate—for that is what it was.

• In Philadelphia was David Franks, son of Jacob, of New York. David was the Franks' agent for the state or colony of Pennsylvania. He was at the seat of the colonial government, the center of American politics. He was hand in glove with many of the fathers of the American Government. He was an immensely rich man (although but an agent) and carried a high hand at Philadelphia.

• At Montreal was another Franks—David Solesbury Franks—also in the business of army contractor. He was a gay young man, described as "a blooded buck," who knew all the arts of turning an "honest" penny out of the needs of armies and the distress of nations. This young man was a grandson or grandnephew of the Moses Franks of England, as he was a nephew of the David Franks of Philadelphia.

Ford Explains the Importance of a Free Press

"As the propagandists in the United States cannot be trusted to give the people all the facts—even though these propagandists have the facts in their possession—it devolves upon some impartial agency to do so. Jewish propagandists in particular are accorded the utmost freedom of the newspapers of the United States—by reason of Jewish advertising being more than 75% of all the advertising done in this country—and thus a wide web of false impressions is constantly being woven around the Jewish Question. The most recent is the widespread publication of a new 'exposure' of the origin of the *Protocols* [*of the Learned Elders of Zion*]. This makes the sixth 'final' and 'complete' exposure that has been put forth for public consumption. . . . It is *The Dearborn Independent*'s purpose to open up from time to time new angles of the Jewish Question, so that the candid reader who would be informed of the extensive character of Jewish influence may obtain a general view of it." (Above, Ford, the author of the accompanying article, works on a V-8 engine.—Ed.)

Here and there were other Franks, all intent on business with the government, but the four here mentioned carry along the main parts of the tale.

A moment's digression will give us at once a view of the looseness of the liberalism of some of the Fathers of the Country, and a view of the equanimity with which David Franks of Philadelphia could pass from one role to another—a facility that cost him dearly when war came on.

John Trumbull, an artist of considerable note at the time, whose paintings still adorn the national Capitol, was invited to dine at Thomas Jefferson's home, among the guests being Sen. Giles, from Virginia. Trumbull tells the story:

> I was scarcely seated when [Mr.] Giles began to [rail] me on the Puritanical ancestry and character of New England. I saw there was no other person from New England present, and, therefore, although conscious that I was in no degree qualified to manage a religious discussion, I felt myself bound to defend my country on this delicate point as well as I could. Whether it had been prearranged that a debate on the Christian religion, in which it should be powerfully ridiculed on the one side and weakly defended on the other, was to be brought forward as promising amusement to a rather free-thinking dinner party, I will not presume to say, but it had that appearance, and Giles pushed his raillery, to my no small annoyance, if not to my discomfiture, until dinner was announced.
>
> That, I hoped, would relieve me by giving a new turn to the conversation, but the company was hardly seated at the table when he renewed the assault with increased asperity, and proceeded so far at last as to ridicule the character, conduct and doctrines of the Divine Founder of our religion; Mr. Jefferson in the meantime smiling and nodding approval on Mr. Giles, while the rest of the company silently left me and my defense to our fate, until at length my friend David Franks took up the argument on my side. Thinking this a fair opportunity for avoiding further conversation on the subject, I turned to Mr. Jefferson and said, "Sir, this is a strange situation in which I find myself; in a country professing Christianity and at a table with Christians, as I supposed, I find my religion and myself attacked with severe and almost irresistible wit and raillery, and not a person to aid in my defense but my friend Mr. Franks, who is himself a Jew."

A series of battles in September and October 1777 were decisive American victories in the Revolutionary War, resulting in the surrender of a British army comprising over 6,000 men invading New York from Canada. Known as the "Battle of Saratoga," this battle was actually two battles fought 18 days apart, but on the same ground, nine miles south of Saratoga, New York. The engagements are known as the Battle of Freeman's Farm (Sept. 19) and the Battle of Bemis Heights (October 7). It was in this second engagement (shown above) that Arnold disobeyed orders to remain in his tent and rallied faltering Colonial troops. This victory forced Gen. John Burgoyne's surrender about a week later. Arnold was, according to reports, dashing from position to position, giving orders his subordinates said helped save the day. Above, Arnold (on rearing horse) led the charge on a key British redoubt at Bemis Heights, and received the injury that effectively ended his career as a fighting man. However, Gen. George Washington did offer Arnold command of half the existing army after Gen. Horatio Gates fully disgraced himself after gaining command of the Continental Army in the South. Arnold turned down that command, requesting instead command of the fort at West Point, New York. Above, Arnold at the Battle of Bemis Heights.

This episode throws a curious light on the character of Thomas Jefferson's "philosophical unbelief," the unlovely fashion of that day; it also illustrates a certain facility in David Franks.

Relations between the Colonies and the "mother country" became strained. Political feelings ran high. The lines of division between "American" and "British" began to appear for the first time. At first there was a degree of agreement among all the population, except the government officials, that a protest against governmental abuses was justified and that strong representations should be made in behalf of the Colonists. Even loyalists and imperialists agreed with that. It was a question of domestic politics. But when presently the idea of protest began to develop into the idea of rebellion and independence, a cleavage came. It was one thing to correct the empire, another thing to desert it. Here is where the people of the Colonies split.

ROYALIST LOYALIST

Mr. Jacob Franks [was] royalist and loyalist. New York was, of course, royalist and loyalist. As army contractor for the British government, he had no choice.

Mr. David Franks, down in Philadelphia, was a little nearer the heart of the new American sentiment and could not be so royal and loyal as was his kinsman [to the] north. In fact, David Franks tried to do what is modernly called "the straddle," attempting to side with the empire and with the Colonies, too. It was natural. His business was in Philadelphia. He may also have wished to remain as long as possible in the position of a spy, and send information of the state of public feeling to the royalists. Moreover, he was received in good society and his reputation for wealth and shrewdness won him attentions he could not otherwise have commanded.

So, in 1765 we find him joining the merchants of Philadelphia in the pact not to import articles from England while the hated Stamp Act was in force. In 1775 he favors the continuance of the Colonial currency. He was enjoying his accustomed life in the city—and his acquaintance with the Shippen family, into which the dashing young Benedict Arnold married.

There is a strange intermingling of all the tragic figures of the play: Benedict Arnold marries the girl for whom Major John André wrote a parlor play. Major André, during his period of captivity as an American prisoner of war and before his exchange, was often at the home of David Franks. And David Solesbury Franks, at his post as agent of the Franks syndicate at Montreal, is placed

"Hang the rest of you on a gibbet."

Benedict Arnold's courage, discipline and military brilliance were established, ironically, during a disastrous joint attack on Quebec in the winter of 1775. Arnold, who was now a colonel, and his forces attacked from one side of the city, while Brigadier General Richard Montgomery attacked from the other. While attacking, Arnold was wounded in the ankle, but he stayed in the battle, organizing troops. Two years later, at the second battle of Saratoga, Bemis Heights, October 7, 1777, Arnold was shot in the same leg, under the buttocks. The leg was then broken when Arnold's horse landed on him after being hit with a musket ball. As a result he had a limp for the rest of his days. A monument to Arnold's leg (shown above) now stands at Saratoga battlefield, though his name was intentionally left off. Later, upon switching sides to fight for the British, Arnold fought a number of successful battles, going so far as to capture Richmond. Arnold supposedly asked a captured colonial officer what the Americans would do if they captured him. The captain is said to have replied: "Cut off your leg, bury it with full military honors, and then hang the rest of you on a gibbet."

by a strange turn of the wheel of destiny in the military family of Benedict Arnold for a considerable period preceding and including the great treason.

So, for the moment let us leave the Jewish family of Franks—all of them still stationed as we first described them: Moses in England, Jacob at New York, David at Philadelphia, David S. at Montreal—and let us scrutinize the young American officer Benedict Arnold.

These facts would most of them be lost, had they not been preserved in the Jewish archives, by the American Jewish Historical Society. You will read any history of Benedict Arnold without perceiving the Jews around him. The authors of the accepted histories were blind.

The principal defect in Arnold's character was his love of money. All of the trouble that led up to the situation in which he found himself with reference to the American government and Army, was due to the suspicion that hung like a cloud over many of his business transactions. There have been attempts to paint Arnold as a martyr, as one who was discouraged by the unmerited slights of the Continental Congress, as a victim of the jealousy of lesser men, as one from whom confidence was unjustly withheld. Nothing could be further from the facts. He was a man to whom men were instinctively drawn to be generous, but so general was the knowledge of his looseness in money matters that, while admiring him, his brother officers acted upon the [self-]protective instinct and held aloof from him. He was tainted by a low form of dishonesty before he was tainted with treason, and the chief explanation of his treason was in the hard bargain he drove as to the amount of money he was to receive for his guilty act.

Arnold's own record makes this clear. Let us then take up his career at a certain point and see how the "Franks strand" and the "money strand" weave themselves through it like colored threads.

EXTRAORDINARY EFFORTS

Extraordinary efforts have been made in recent years to extenuate Arnold's treason by the recital of his daring services. These services need not be minimized. Indeed, it was his great achievement of the winter march to Montreal and Quebec in 1775-6 that seems to begin the chapter of his troubles. To rehearse this feat of courage and endurance would be to tell a tale that has thrilled the American schoolboy.

It was at Montreal that Benedict Arnold came into contact with the young Jew, David Solesbury Franks, the Canadian agent of the Franks army purveying syndicate. And the next thing known about young Franks is that he returns to the American Colonies in the train of Benedict Arnold as an officer of the American Army.

How this change was effected is not explained in any of the records. There is a moment of darkness, as it were, in which the "quick change" was made, which transformed the young man from Montreal from an army contractor for the British into an officer of Arnold's staff.

But as it is impossible for every fact to be suppressed. There are here and there indications of what might have been, what indeed most probably was, the basis of the attraction and relations between the two. It was very probably—almost certainly—the opportunities for graft which could be capitalized by a combination of Gen. Arnold's authority and young Franks's ability in the handling of goods.

From the day they met in Montreal until the hour when Gen. Arnold fled, a traitor, from the fort on the Hudson, young David Solesbury Franks was his companion.

In one of the numerous courts-martial that tried Gen. Arnold for questionable dealings in matters pertaining to Army supplies, Franks, who was aide-de-camp to Arnold, and by rank a major, testified thus: "I had, by being in the Army, injured my private affairs very considerably and meant to leave it, if a proper opportunity of entering into business should happen. I had several conversations on the subject with Gen. Arnold, who promised me all the assistance in his power; he was to participate in the profits of the business I was to enter in."

This testimony was given by Maj. Franks in 1779; the two men had met in the winter of 1775-6, but, as the records will show, Maj. Franks was always Gen. Arnold's reliance on getting out of scrapes caused by questionable business methods in which Arnold's military authority was used quite freely. Maj. Franks admits that he was to enter business and Gen. Arnold was to share the profits. On what basis this arrangement could exist, is another point not known. Arnold had no capital. He had no credit. He was a spendthrift, a borrower, notorious for his constant need of money. The only credible inducement for Franks to accept a partnership with him was on the understanding that Arnold should use his military authority to throw business to Franks. Or, to state it more bluntly, the "profits" Benedict Arnold was to receive were payments for his misuse of authority for his own gain.

It was at Montreal that Arnold's name first became tainted with rumors of shady dealing in private and public property. Gen. George Washington had

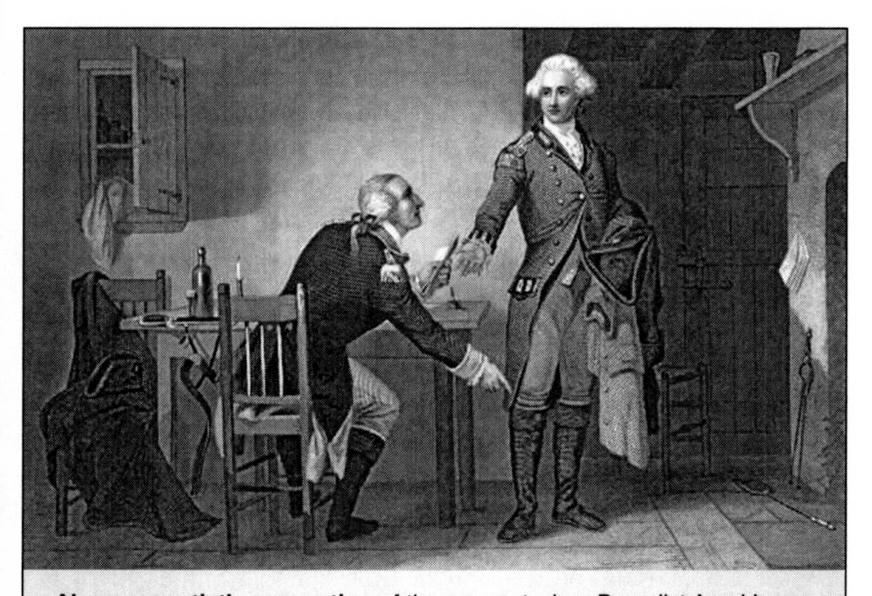

Above, an artist's conception of the moment when Benedict Arnold gave Major John André his secret communication for the British detailing the defenses of West Point. Arnold is shown pointing to André's boot. It was in André's boot that the secret communique was found by colonial militiamen when André was stopped, ostensibly to be robbed. André was later hanged. Arnold, on the other hand, escaped (below) to his personal barge that would take him to the British sloop *Vulture*, and safety from the Americans.

laid down the most explicit instructions on these matters, with a view to having the Canadians treated as fellow-Americans and not as enemies. Gen. Washington had cashiered officers and whipped soldiers who had previously disobeyed the order against looting and theft.

Gen. Arnold had seized large quantities of goods at Montreal and had hurried them away without making proper accounting of them. This he admits in his letter to Gen. Schuyler: "Our hurry and confusion was so great when the goods were received, it was impossible to take a particular account of them." This means only that Arnold seized the goods without giving the Canadian citizens proper receipts for them, so that he had in his hands a large amount of wealth for which he was under no compulsion to account to anybody. This mass of goods he sent to Col. Hazen at Chambley, and Colonel Hazen, evidently aware of the conditions under which the goods were taken, refused to receive them. This disobedience of Col. Hazen to his superior officer, especially in a question relating to goods, made it necessary for Arnold to take some self-protective action, which he did in his letter to Gen. Schuyler. Meantime, a very ugly rumor ran through the American Army that Gen. Benedict Arnold had tried to pull a scurvy trick of graft, but had been held up by the strict conduct of Col. Hazen.

Moreover, it was rumored (and the fact was admitted by Arnold in his letter) that in the transfer the goods were well sorted over so that when they finally arrived a great part of them was missing.

All the principal facts were admitted by Arnold, who used them, however, to throw blame on Col. Hazen. He even went so far as to prepare charges against Col. Hazen, forcing the matter into a court-martial. The court was called and refused to hear the witnesses chosen by Gen. Arnold on his behalf, on the ground that the witnesses were not entitled to credibility. Whereupon Gen. Arnold flouted the court, who ordered him arrested. Gen. Gates, to preserve the useful services of Arnold to the United States Army, dissolved the court-martial, to that extent condoning the conduct of Arnold. Before the court-martial ended, however, it informally acquitted Col. Hazen.

Here then, almost immediately, as it would seem, upon his new connection with David Solesbury Franks, Benedict Arnold is involved in a bad tangle concerning property which had come into his possession irregularly and which disappeared soon after. His attempt to throw the blame on an officer whose disobedience was the factor that disclosed the true state of affairs, failed. It was his bold scheme to forestall an exposure which must inevitably have come.

While it is true that on this Montreal case, no verdict stands recorded against Benedict Arnold for the theft of goods, it is also true that the American Army became suspicious of him from that day.

Had Arnold been innocent then and had he kept his hands clean thereafter, the Montreal episode would have been forgotten. But as a matter of fact such affairs came with increasing frequency thereafter, all of them, strangely enough, involving the same man whom he associated with himself at the time of that first exposure. The story of this man's relations with Arnold all through the period ending with the great treason, may now be taken up with greater consecutiveness, for now their formerly separate courses run together.

NOTE: This article first appeared in the March/April 2009 issue of the bimonthly historical journal The Barnes Review. TBR is $46 for one year. Call 1-877-773-9077 toll free to order or visit www.barnesreview.com.

Benedict Arnold's Letter to the Inhabitants of America

CONTRARY TO POPULAR BELIEF, Benedict Arnold cared about what the American people thought of him. What follows is the full text of Arnold's "Letter to the Inhabitants of America," in which he lays out the reasons he betrayed the Colonial cause—and his good friend, George Washington—and took up arms for the king of England.

BY BENEDICT ARNOLD

I should forfeit, even in my own opinion, the place I have so long held in yours, if I could be indifferent to your approbation, and silent on the motives which have induced me to join the King's arms. A very few words, however, shall suffice upon a subject so personal; for to the thousands who suffer under the tyranny of the usurpers in the revolted provinces, as well as to the great multitude who have long wished for its subversion, this instance of my conduct can want no vindication; and as to the class of men who are criminally protracting the war from sinister views at the expense of the public interest, I prefer their enmity to their applause.

I am, therefore, only concerned in this address, to explain, myself to such of my countrymen, as want abilities, or opportunities, to detect the artifices by which they are duped.

Having fought by your side when the love of our country animated our arms, I shall expect, from your justice and candor, what your deceivers, with more art and less honesty, will find it inconsistent with their own views to admit. When I quitted domestic happiness for the perils of the field, I conceived the rights of my country in danger, and that duty and honor called me to her defense. A redress of grievances was my only object and aim; however, I acquiesced in a step which I thought [precipitous], the declaration of independence: to justify this measure, many plausible reasons were urged, which could no longer exist, when Great Britain, with the open arms of a parent, offered to embrace us as children, and grant the wished-for redress.

And now that her worst enemies are in in her own bosom, I should change my principles, if I conspired with their designs; yourselves being judges, was the war less just, because fellow subjects were considered as our foe? You have felt the torture in which we raised arms against a brother. God incline the guilty protectors of these unnatural dissensions to resign their ambition, and cease from their delusion, in compassion to kindred blood!

I anticipate your question, Was not the war a defensive one, until the French joined in the combination? I answer, that I thought so. You will add, Was it not afterwards necessary, till the separation of the British empire was complete? By no means; in contending for the welfare of my country, I am free to declare my opinion, that this end attained, all strife should have ceased.

I lamented, therefore, the impolicy, tyranny, and injustice, which, with a sovereign contempt of the people of America, studiously neglected to take their collective sentiments of the British proposals of peace, and to negotiate, under a suspension of arms, for an adjustment of differences; I lamented it as a dangerous sacrifice of the great interests of this country to the partial views of a proud, ancient, and crafty foe. I had my suspicions of some imperfections in our councils, on proposals prior to the Parliamentary Commission of 1778; but having then less to do in the Cabinet than the field (I will not pronounce peremptorily, as some may, and perhaps justly, that Congress have veiled them from the public eye), I continued to be guided in the negligent confidence of a Soldier. But the whole world saw, and all Americans confessed, that the overtures of the second Commission exceeded our wishes and expectations; and if there was any suspicion of the national liberality, it arose from its excess.

Do any [believe] we were at that time really entangled by an alliance with France? Unfortunate deception! They have been duped, by a virtuous credulity, in the incautious moments of intemperate passion, to give up their felicity to serve a nation wanting both the will and the power to protect us, and aiming at the destruction both of the mother country and the provinces. In the plainness of common sense, for I pretend to no casuistry, did the pretended treaty with the Court of Versailles, amount to more than an overture to America? Certainly not, because no authority had been given by the people to conclude it, nor to this very hour have they authorized its ratification. The articles of confederation remain still unsigned.

In the firm persuasion, therefore, that the private judgement of an individual citizen of this country is as free from all conventional restraints, since as before the insidious offers of France, I preferred those from Great Britain; thinking it infinitely wiser and safer to cast my confidence upon her justice and generosity, than to trust a monarchy too feeble to establish your independency, so perilous to her distant dominions; the enemy of the Protestant faith and fraudulently avowing an affection for the liberties of mankind, while she holds her native sons in vassalage and chains.

I affect no disguise, and therefore frankly declare, that in these principles I had determined to retain my arms and command for an opportunity to surrender them to Great Britain; and in concerting the measures for a purpose, in my opinion, as grateful as it would have been beneficial to my country; I was only solicitous to accomplish an event of decisive importance, and to prevent as much as possible, in the execution of it, the effusion of blood.

With the highest satisfaction I bear testimony to my old fellow soldiers and citizens, that I find solid ground to rely upon the clemency of our Sovereign, and abundant conviction that it is the generous intention of Great Britain not only to leave the rights and privileges of the colonies unimpaired, together with their perpetual exemption from taxation, but to superadd such further benefits as may consist with the common prosperity of the empire. In short, I fought for much less than the parent country is willing to grant to her colonies as they can be to receive or enjoy.

Some may think I continued in the struggle of these unhappy days too long, and others that I quitted it much too soon.

To the first I reply, that I did not see with their eyes, nor perhaps had so favorable a situation to look from, and that to our common master I am willing to stand or fall. In behalf of the candid among the latter, some of whom I believe serve blindly—but honestly—in the bands I have left, I pray God to give them all the lights requisite to their own safety before it is too late; and with respect to that herd of censurers, whose enmity to me originates in their hatred to the principles by which I am now led to devote my life to the re-union of the British empire, as the best and only means to dry up the streams of misery that have deluged this country, they may be assured, that conscious of the rectitude of my intentions; I shall treat their malice and calumnies with contempt and neglect. ✦

B. Arnold, New York, October 7, 1780

At left, a painting of Col. Banastre Tarleton by English artist Sir Joshua Reynolds. On May 29, 1780, Tarleton defeated Col. Abraham Buford at the Waxhaws, and bayoneted the wounded, thus creating the American battle cry "Tarleton's quarter." Tarleton soon became the most hated man in the British military, from an American view.

Banastre Tarleton:

Did he really deserve the moniker "Bloody Ban"?

By Paul T. Angel

In the movie *The Patriot*, starring Mel Gibson, which related (or was loosely based upon) the heroic life of Francis "Swamp Fox" Marion, as told through the fictional tale of widower-farmer Benjamin Martin, British Col. Banastre Tarleton (1754-1833) is portrayed as a ruthless and cruel military officer. Historians, however, remain divided as to whether the leader of several regiments of dragoons deserved his notorious reputation or whether he was simply fighting to win in a bloody guerrilla-style war.[1]

During the American Revolution, numerous lengthy battles were fought wherein soldiers engaged in hand-to-hand combat and stained many a farmer's field with blood. It was all-out war, and civilians as well regularly became targets as cities were turned into battlefields and neighbors were pitted against neighbors.

In the so-called Waxhaw Massacre (see accompanying story), which lasted 15 minutes, historians contend Tarleton's forces most likely killed about a third of Buford's men and wounded another third. When compared to other massacres carried out by revolutionary forces, such as the infamous Pyle's Hacking Match, wherein the forces of Lt. Col. Henry "Light Horse Harry" Lee and Capt. Joseph Graham, with their green uniforms, were mistaken for British dragoons (who also wore green uniforms) and proceeded to slaughter a force of Loyalists (about 90 were killed, while the Patriots lost just one horse), one could argue that Tarleton was merely fighting in a very messy war. (Pyle's 1781 Hacking Match, or "Pyle's Defeat," is named for Col. John Pyle.)

After acquiring the nickname "Ban the Butcher" at Waxhaws, Tarleton became renowned for his frustration in trying to combat Marion, who was successfully waging irregular war against British forces in South Carolina. To win the hearts and minds of townspeople, many of whom were torn between supporting the Patriots and staying out of the war, Revolutionary fighters regularly embellished stories about Tarleton and his men to use as a rallying cry. One incident, as related by one of Marion's men, William Dobein James, stands out:

> On one expedition (Nelson's Ferry, November 1780), Tarleton burnt the house, outhouses, corn and fodder, and a great part of the cattle, hogs and poultry, of the estate of Gen. Richardson. The general had been active with the Americans, but was now dead; and the British leader, in civilized [sic] times, made his widow and children suffer for the deeds of the husband and parent, after the manner of the East [Orient], and [the] coast of Barbary. What added to the cruel nature of the act was that he had first dined in the house, and helped himself to the abundant good cheer it afforded. But we have seen before the manner in which he requited hospitality. It was generally observed of Tarleton and his corps, that they not only exercised more acts of cruelty than anyone in the British army, but also carried further the spirit of depredation.[2]

Was this story real, or was it another exaggeration used to provoke rage against the British occupiers?

Today, there is no dispute that Tarleton was certainly a masterful cavalry leader. At one point, he nearly succeeded in capturing the patriot governor of Virginia, Thomas Jefferson, in a daring raid on Charlottesville, Va.

Unlike his character in *The Patriot*, Tarleton survived the American Revolution and eventually returned to England, where he was lauded for his service and was promoted to general.

So did he deserve his reputation? Apparently, that depends which side you were fighting on. ✦

ENDNOTES:

1 For more on Francis "Swamp Fox" Marion, see THE BARNES REVIEW, July/August 2003.

2 *The Life of Brig. Gen. Francis Marion*, by Gen. Peter Horry and M.L. Weems. First published in 1824.

PAUL T. ANGEL is the managing editor of THE BARNES REVIEW historical magazine. He is trained as a graphic designer and art historian. He received his Bachelor's Degree in Design in 1983 from American University in Washington, D.C. He has a keen interest—with a particular focus—on the study of evidence indicating that ancient Europeans made it to the shores of America thousands of years before Columbus. His articles on the ancient megalithic monuments found throughout New England, published in the November and December 1997 issues of TBR, have been reproduced on more than 200 websites.

NOTE: This article first appeared in the March/April 2009 issue of the bimonthly historical journal THE BARNES REVIEW. TBR is $46 for one year. Call 1-877-773-9077 toll free to order or visit www.barnesreview.com.

Quantrill:

Psychopathic Killer or Avenging Angel?

AUGUST 21, 2007 WAS THE 144TH ANNIVERSARY of William Clarke Quantrill's Lawrence Raid of 1863. The raid has been the subject of much debate ever since. Many mainstream historians have portrayed him and his men as ruthless, psychopathic, bloodthirsty killers. When the facts are reviewed, one sees that most of these Missourians were patriots, fighting for their homes and families. They were no different than the patriots of the American Revolution, and the only line of defense left in Missouri against Socialist Marxists who were doing the bidding of Abraham Lincoln. When the full story is told, one learns that Quantrill exercised much restraint upon his men in Lawrence. Orders were given that no women or children were to be harmed. In review of the facts, it is revealed that Kansas Sen. James Lane's raid on Osceola, Missouri, two years prior, was four times as destructive. The straw that broke the camel's back was the intentional collapse of a makeshift jail in Kansas City, Missouri, that held many female relatives of the Rebel guerrillas—some of them as young as 10 years old.

BY CLINT E. LACY

Historian James McPherson in his book *Battle Cry of Freedom* described William Quantrill and the Partisan Rangers he commanded as: "some of the most psychopathic killers in American history."

McPherson goes on to describe Quantrill's Raid on Lawrence, Kansas on August 21, 1863, as follows:

> Four hundred and fifty men under Quantrill (including the Younger brothers and Frank James) headed for Lawrence, Kansas, the hated center of "free soilism" since Bleeding Kansas days. After crossing the Kansas line they kidnapped ten farmers to guide them toward Lawrence and murdered each after his usefulness was over. Approaching the town at dawn on August 21, Quantrill ordered his followers: Kill every male and burn

every house. They almost did. The first to die was a United Brethren clergyman, shot through the head while he sat milking his cow. During the next three hours Quantrill's band murdered another 182 men and boys and burned 185 buildings in Lawrence. They rode out of town ahead of pursuing Union cavalry and, after a harrowing chase, made it back to their Missouri sanctuary, where they scattered to the woods.[1]

QUANTRILL & HIS RAIDERS

Unfortunately, this account by McPherson is widely accepted as fact by many of his contemporaries and the public at large. When the facts are reviewed, however; one learns that Quantrill was no psychopath, nor were the men who followed him.

Quantrill and the men who rode with him, and in similar guerrilla units, were officially given the term Partisan Rangers. Historian Paul R. Peterson gives a more sober account about Missouri during the War of Northern Aggression, the formation of Missouri's Partisan Ranger organization and a detailed history of Quantrill in his book *Quantrill of Missouri* (2003, Cumberland House Publishing).

Peterson writes that following Confederate Gen. Sterling Price's victories at Wilson's Creek and Lexington, Missouri:

> Price's army pulled back and marched South toward Arkansas. . . . Winter was not far off, and Price realized that he would not be able to feed and supply his men in winter quarters. The situation was also affected by the short enlistment terms of most of Price's soldiers. Many three-month enlistments had already expired. An alternative, which the general endorsed as a military necessity, was to establish groups of Partisan Rangers. Partisans protected their own land and provided for themselves. Organized, independent ranger companies would keep Union forces in the state occupied and off balance.

A fast, well-armed, mobile force existing off the land and supported by friends and family could do more damage to a Federal Army of occupation than Price could by trying to maneuver a numerically superior adversary into a desirable site for battle. Price knew that his army required an intelligence network, and the guerrillas could set themselves up in every county and locale. At the same time, partisans could disrupt the enemy's supply lines and communication."[2]

According to the Missouri Partisan Ranger website:

The above illustration first appeared in *Harper's Weekly* magazine on September 5, 1863. The caption read: "The Destruction of the City of Lawrence, Kansas, and the Massacre of its Inhabitants by the Rebel Guerrillas, August, 21, 1863." Lawrence was an important stop on the Underground Railroad and the base for many Abolitionist organizations which made it a target for pro-slavery groups. But what the pro-North history books fail to tell you is key to understanding the whole story. First, the attack on Lawrence was inspired by a brutal Jayhawker attack on Osceola, Missouri, in which Northern partisans purposefully caused a building to collapse on imprisoned Missourian women and children. Second, according to witnesses, Quantrill demanded that no women or children be harmed. This command was obeyed at Lawrence.

Confederate States President Jefferson Davis did not believe in guerrilla warfare, considering it too disorganized. However, on April 21, 1862 he approved an act to authorize commissioned officers to form bands of Partisan rangers. It was then that General Thomas C. Hindman published his "Confederate Partisan Act in Missouri." Hindman believed fully in the military value of guerrilla warfare. General Hindman's "Confederate Partisan Act in Missouri" was issued from his headquarters of the Trans-Mississippi Department in Little Rock Arkansas on July 17, 1862. The following is the glorious, official order recognizing the importance of the Missouri Partisan Ranger:

CONFEDERATE PARTISAN ACT IN MISSOURI

I. For the more effectual annoyance of the enemy upon our rivers and in our mountains and woods, all citizens of this district who are not conscripted are called upon to organize themselves into independent companies of mounted men or infantry, as they prefer, arming themselves and to serve in that part of the district to which they belong.

II. When as many as 10 men come together for this purpose they may organize by electing a captain, 1 sergeant, 1 corporal, and will at once commence operations against the enemy without waiting for special instructions. Their duty will be to cut off Federal pickets, scouts, foraging parties and trains and to kill pilots and others on gunboats and transports, attacking them day and night and using the greatest vigor in their movements. As soon as the company attains the strength required by law it will proceed to elect the other officers to which it is entitled. All such organizations will be reported to their headquarters as soon as practicable. They will receive pay and allowances for subsistence and forage for the time actually in the field, as established by the affidavits of their captains.

III. These companies will be governed in all respects by the same regulations as other troops. Captains will be held responsible for the good conduct and efficiency of their men and will report to these headquarters from time to time.

—Gen. Thomas C. Hindman[3]

REASONS FOR THE RAID

Today, modern-day court historians, media outlets and public education institutions are quick to call Quantrill's raid on Lawrence, Kansas a "massacre." However; there were two primary reasons for Quantrill's raid on the Eastern Kansas abolitionist stronghold. The first involves operations being conducted by Sen. James Lane's Kansas Jayhawkers.

As Gen. Price was moving North toward Lexington, following his victory at Wilson's Creek, James Lane and his men were following cautiously behind him plundering Missouri farms and harassing citizens from a safe distance. Once again quoting Peterson:

> While Price's army was closing on Lexington, rather than render assistance to Mulligan, Lane and his ragtag army of 1,200 Kansas Jayhawkers marched instead against the small pro-Southern town of Osceola, Missouri, in St. Clair County.
>
> The Missouri editor of the *Weston Argus* described the sight of 50

shiftless horsemen riding through his town to join "Lane's Brigade."

They were nearly naked, and minus shoes and hats in many cases. They were not armed, but a number of them had hams of meat on their backs, which they no doubt had stolen from some man's meat house on the road. These are the kind of men that Lane's Brigade is to be composed of: thieves, cutthroats, and midnight robbers. These hirelings passed through town in a full trot, their eyes looking as big as new moons, as they expected at every corner to be stopped or fired on by the Rebels. On a dark night such soldiers would make a splendid charge on a hen-roost, meat house, negro kitchen or stable, but they can't fight honest Americans in daylight.[4]

LOOTERS TARGETED

This description of the men who belonged to "Lane's Brigade" provided by Peterson, via the writings of a newspaper editor, paint a vivid portrait of New England Puritans, who immigrated to Kansas in pursuit of a socialist utopia that ultimately left them desolate and hungry. Jim Lane and his "Kansas Brigade" no doubt had a far greater prize in mind than the "hen-roost, meat house and negro kitchen":

Osceola was one of the more prosperous towns in southwest Missouri. At the beginning of the war, the population was greater than 3,000. . . . On September 23, 1861, when Lane entered the area, there wasn't a Confederate soldier within miles of the town. With Lane were Col. William Wir's Fourth Kansas Jayhawker Regiment and Col. James Montgomery's Third Kansas Jayhawker Regiment. A few residents fired on the Jayhawkers so Lane ordered Capt. Thomas Moonlight to shell the town.

After the Union guns had receded the town to rubble, nine male inhabitants were brought to the town square for a drumhead court-martial and shot. Most of the remaining residents were women and children. Banks were an easy target for the Jayhawkers, but the Osceola bank prudently had shipped its funds elsewhere. When Lane found little currency in the bank, he ordered the stores, warehouses and homes ransacked. His men loaded the lot into government wagons and any other vehicles they could confiscate. Among Lane's personal haul were a number of pianos for his home in Lawrence.

He then set the town afire. Of Osceola's 800 buildings all but three were turned to ashes. No consideration was given to political leanings of the homeowners. The plunder included 350 horses, 400 head of cattle, 200 kid-

> napped slaves, 3,000 sacks of flour and 50 sacks of coffee. The Jayhawkers also took the county records from the courthouse. Lane stole a fine carriage from the home of his colleague, U.S. Sen. Waldo P. Johnson, and sent it to his family in Lawrence along with several silk dresses.
>
> Eyewitnesses noted that the plunder train of 150 wagons was at least a mile long. Property losses were estimated at more than $1 million. One jayhawker wrote: As the Sun went down Sunday night Osceola was a heap of smoldering ruins. Three thousand people were left homeless when Osceola was burned, and perhaps the fairest city in Missouri had been utterly wiped from the Earth.[5]
>
> Also worth noting is the fact that Peterson reveals: "The Osceola Raid was four times more destructive than the 1863 Lawrence Raid."[6]

If Lawrence, Kansas, represented a failed socialist utopia, then no doubt those who lived there looked resentfully across the border at Osceola, a symbol of Southern culture, free trade, capitalism and prosperity carved out of the Missouri timberline.

Prior to the election of Lincoln and the subsequent invasion of their state by the Union army, Missourians were able to keep the envious Kansans in line. But as the war between Northern and Southern ideals collided, Missourians soon found that they could no longer keep Kansas and its Jayhawkers in check, while simultaneously trying to drive back invading hordes from Iowa, Minnesota, Wisconsin and Illinois as well.

CLAIM MORAL HIGH GROUND

Jayhawkers such as Lane, Montgomery and Jennison could now legitimize their attacks by wrapping themselves in the Union cause and claiming a "moral high ground" of fighting for the freedom of the slaves. This too was a myth. Jayhawkers had no problem stealing from or abusing Negroes. Many of the slaves taken from Osceola soon found themselves in a different land, doing the same work for different masters. Their benevolent "liberators" now utilized them to harvest their wheat fields.

The captured slaves were taken into Kansas and assigned to farmers to work in the wheat fields. Their pay was anything they could steal and carry away from their former owners and sell in public-street auctions in the towns where they were taken.

During the autumn of 1861, Kansas farmers prized the slaves brought out of Missouri by the Lane Brigade. *The Lawrence Journal*, however, accused Lane of requiring payment from the farmers for providing them. Almost two years later

The Leavenworth Daily Conservative affirmed that "the large crop of 1863 was made possible only by negro hands. . . . Almost every farm is supplied with labor in the shape of one or two large, healthy negroes."[7]

Following General Price's withdrawal from Missouri, Sen. James Lane moved his brigade to an encampment outside of Kansas City. Seymour D. Thompson described Lane as: "The last man we would have taken as a general. He had on citizen's pants, a soldier's blouse, and a dilapidated white hat. He rolled under his dark brows a pair of piercing eyes."[8]

AS INSANE AS EMPEROR NERO

A *New York Times* reporter described Lane as: "a Joe Bagstock Nero fiddling and laughing over the burning of some Missouri Rome."[9]

No doubt Lane, the "Grim Chieftain," was smug in knowing that now the Missourians and their culture of capitalism, free trade and prosperity were destitute. No longer were the Southern culture and Jeffersonian philosophies of Missouri superior to the failed socialist policies of Kansas and its Puritan Yankees. It too had failed its citizens, with a little help from Lane and his Kansas Jayhawker Brigade and the administration of Abraham Lincoln, who legitimized them.

Following Lane's attack and destruction of Osceola, Missouri, many of his Union commanders called for this kind of blatant destruction and looting to stop: "Maj. W.E. Prince, in Leavenworth, learned about Lane's depredations, and wrote him that he hoped the looting might be stopped. Gov. Robinson appealed directly to Gen. Fremont."[10]

Earlier that year, Abraham Lincoln in a letter to Simon Cameron had nothing but praise for Lane, writing that:

> I have been reflecting upon the subject, and have concluded that we need the service of such a man out there at once; that we had better appoint him a brigadier-general of volunteers today, and send him off . . . to raise a force (I think two regiments better than three, but as to this I am not particular) as you think will get him into actual work quickest.[11]

Due to the actions of men like Lane toward Missouri citizens, Gen. Price's plan to form Partisan Ranger units soon became a resounding success. In fact, many men who followed Price into Confederate service began to leave and return to Missouri so that they could become Partisans as well. As early as 1863 the Confederate Government viewed Missouri as "lost." General Price himself had demanded that the Missourians be sent back West of the Mississippi, or he too would return to his home state and "bushwhack it."[12]

'FEDERALS' MISCALCULATE

In his book, *Bushwhackers of the Border*, Missouri author and historian Patrick Brophy writes:

> Price's successes [in 1861] had forced the Federals to revise their own strategy, settling for humbler objectives. Conceding the Southwest for the time being, they would focus on holding the vital jugular of the Missouri-Mississippi, along the long oxbow line of Cape Girardeau-Rolla-Sedalia-Kansas City—the Border. But they were reckoning without the guerrillas. As 1862 came, insurgent activity goaded them back onto the offensive.[13]

The Partisan Rangers were successful at defending their homes and harassing Union occupational troops. They were unfairly credited with the policy of "no quarter," or taking no prisoners. Years after the war many former Partisans while recounting their war experiences noted that Partisans considered themselves soldiers, and behaved as such, that is until Henry Halleck issued the first "no quarter" policy of the war.

In an article entitled "Quantrill: Soldier or Murderer?" Martin Kelley writes:

> Quantrill and his men staged numerous raids into Kansas during the early part of the Civil War. He was quickly labeled an outlaw by the Union for his attacks on pro-Union forces. He was involved in several skirmishes with Jayhawkers (pro-Union guerrilla bands) and eventually was made a captain in the Confederate Army. His attitude toward his role in the Civil War drastically changed in 1862 when the commander of the Department of Missouri, Major General Henry W. Halleck ordered that guerrillas such as Quantrill and his men would be treated as robbers and murderers, not normal prisoners of war. Before this proclamation, Quantrill acted as if he were a normal soldier adhering to principles of accepting enemy surrender. After this, he gave an order to give "no quarter."[14]

As Missouri Partisan John McCorkle once wrote: "We tried to fight like soldiers but were declared outlaws, hunted under a black flag and murdered like beasts."[15]

CIVILIAN POLICY

Halleck also had a special policy directed toward civilians. He "sought to run a taut ship, in which everyone in his department, soldier and civilian alike, kept in line. Citizens who manifested support for the enemy could have their property taken through confiscation or contribution."[16] The year 1863 saw a new Union commander to oversee operations in Missouri:

> The decisionmakers in the North began to look for a military leader who could lead them out of the morass of guerrilla warfare. By midsummer they thought they had found such a man: Brig. Gen. Thomas Ewing.[17]

Ewing was the adopted brother and (ironically) a brother-in-law to William Tecumseh Sherman, a Union general who became famous for his own infamous atrocities during the war. It has been said that he was an ambitious man who wanted to be a U.S. senator someday and thought he had a better chance at achieving this goal by gaining favor with James Lane. Perhaps this would explain the actions he would soon conduct in Missouri against civilians, especially women.

Ewing knew the guerrillas were aided by their numerous friends and relatives in the area. On August 13, *The Kansas City Journal* reported that Ewing was at departmental headquarters in St. Louis seeking authorization to banish the families of known guerrillas. From this meeting, five days later, Ewing issued his infamous General Order No. 10.[18]

Order No. 10 required officers to arrest all men and women, not heads of families, who willfully aided "the enemy." It also required that persons who were heads of families who willfully aided the enemy leave his military district.

UNION MURDERED WOMEN AND GIRLS

This leads to the second reason that Missouri Partisans raided Lawrence, Kansas on August 21, 1863:

> Union authorities acting out of frustration for losing most all of their encounters with the guerrillas, decided to banish all Southern[ers] in the area who were helping these men defend their homes. Federal officials issued orders to execute anyone giving aid to the Partisan Rangers.
>
> In the midsummer of July 1863, federal occupational troops began to arrest and detain many area women (mainly those related to Missouri Partisan Rangers) who were said to be spying and gathering food and information for the Partisan Rangers.
>
> Among the women detained were close relatives of prominent Partisan Rangers. These included Mary and Josephine Anderson who were sisters of Bill Anderson. These women were to be detained until arrangements could be made to transport them to St. Louis, where they would be tried.
>
> All the prisoners were incarcerated into a three-story building named the

Union propaganda, showing Southern partisans committing all sorts of despicable acts, was full of historical inaccuracies, yet Northern readers who viewed the illustration in their newspapers knew no better and believed the atrocity stories contained therein. At top right, Confederate partisans take their turn inebriating themselves with pilfered hooch. At top left, several men (one in a striped shirt, smoking) relax while viewing the carnage below. Visible above his friend's head is graffiti that reads: "Death to Yankees" and shows "Old Abe" hanged from a gallows. At far left, a male citizen is hanged and mocked. In the street below, one mean Johnny Reb holds up a baby by the foot and shakes it (reminiscent of the WWI stories about Germans abusing Belgian babies, an atrocity yarn also accepted as fact at the time).

> Longhorn Store and Tavern located on the site of 1409 Grand Ave., Kansas City, Missouri. The Longhorn Store and Tavern was a fairly new structure, and was built in 1856. Awaiting transport, the Longhorn Store and Tavern had been converted into a makeshift jailhouse for women.
>
> On August 13, 1863, the seven-year-old building suddenly collapsed.
>
> Four women were killed including 14-year-old Josephine Anderson, sister of William T. Anderson. Bill's other sister, Mary Anderson, was badly injured (both legs broken).
>
> Also arrested and incarcerated during the collapse were Charity Kerr, sister of John McCorkle (killed), Mrs. Nannie McCorkle, sister-in-law of John McCorkle (uninjured), Susan Vandever, cousin of Cole Younger (killed), Armenia Whitsett Selvey, cousin of Cole Younger (killed).
>
> Here is where the criminal event takes place. . . .
>
> The inner structures and supports of the building were actually weakened by Federal troops so as to make it collapse. Many of the guards had been drinking and celebrating after the collapse, and were overheard bragging and boasting as to the sabotage.[19]

Once again, Paul Peterson's *Quantrill of Missouri* provides an intricately detailed account of this deliberate sabotage. He describes the scene and the building in which the Missouri Partisan's female relatives were being held as follows:

> The unusual construction of the building was that it was actually two separate buildings that shared a common wall as well as floor joists that ran the width of the buildings, almost 50 feet, and rested on the outside walls of both buildings. . . . The soldiers garrisoned in the adjoining guardhouse had examined the building and realized that it could easily be destroyed. A few days prior to August 13, they began to weaken the structure of the Cockrell Building, which they occupied. The soldiers premeditated their designs, known that if they weakened the structural integrity of their own building, it would cause the instability in the adjoining building being used as the female prison.
>
> They began by removing the center posts on the main floor of the guardhouse. This left no support for the roof and the floor joists of their own building, thus creating a lever action and causing the adjoining female prison to collapse on top of their own building.
>
> The soldiers gained access to the basement of the Thomas Building and removed the brick pillars that held up the floor joists of the first floor. . . . Not wanting to injure one of their own men, the assassins next door waited until the lone guard left the prison to fetch the water [that they had sent him

> to get] when they made the final stroke against the supporting column. With the supporting posts and columns in the Cockrell Building finally cut down and removed, the building began to sink. The structure began to fall as the guard was returning. Once the pressure from above started to drive the top stories into the cellar, the supports in the outside walls . . . collapsed on top of the guardhouse.[20]

This alone would be enough to make one thirst for revenge, but upon examination of further details, it makes one wonder why the Missouri Partisans spared Lawrence, Kansas as long as they did. The prisoners included, Charity McCorkle Kerr, Mollie Grinstaff, Martha Anderson, (who at the ripe old age of 10 had angered her Union captors who, in turn, attached a 12-pound ball and chain to her ankle), Molly Anderson, Nannie Harris McCorkle, Susan Crawford Vandever, Armenia Crawford Selvey, and Josephine Anderson.

Peterson writes that after the collapse:

> All but five of the 11 women imprisoned here escaped death. Four were killed immediately . . . [10-year-old] Martha Anderson, restricted by the ball and chain, tried desperately to make it to a window; she lived, but her legs were horribly crushed.[21]

Missouri Partisan John McCorkle, who rode with Quantrill, would later recall:

> This foul murder was the direct cause of the famous raid on Lawrence, Kansas. We could stand no more. Imagine, if you can, my feelings. A loved sister foully murdered and the widow of a dead brother seriously hurt by a set of men whom the name assassins, murderers and cutthroats would be a compliment. . . . The homes of our friends burned, our aged sires, who dared sympathize with us, were either hung or shot in the presence of their families and all their furniture and provisions loaded in wagons and, with our livestock, taken to the state of Kansas.
>
> The beautiful country of Jackson County, Cass County and Johnson County were worse than desert, and on every hillside stood lone blackened chimneys, sad sentinels and monuments to the memory of our once happy homes. And these outrages had been done by Kansas troops, calling themselves soldiers, but a disgrace to the name soldier. And now our innocent and beautiful girls had been murdered in a most foul, brutal, savage and damnable manner. We were determined to have revenge, and so Col.

Quantrill, and Capt. Anderson planned a raid on Lawrence, Kansas, the home of the leaders, Jim Lane and Jennison.[22]

MEN ASSEMBLE

Quantrill soon sent word for his men to assemble at Capt. Perdee's farm on the Blackwater River in Johnson County, Missouri. John Noland, a black scout, accompanied him. Noland wished to participate in the raid but Quantrill had other plans. Quantrill sent first Noland, then Fletch Taylor, to spy on Lawrence. Upon their return, they issued their reports detailing what the Missourians would face there. The reports revealed that Lawrence was lightly defended, and also detailed the amount of plunder, stolen from Missouri, that had been seen there.

Afterward, Quantrill answered questions concerning this raid, then turned to each of his leaders and asked for a vote. The vote from each leader was unanimous, "Lawrence."

According to McCorkle:

> Riding all night, the town was reached at daylight . . . down the main street, shooting at every blue coat that came in sight. Just before entering the town Col. Quantrill turned to his men and said: "Boys, this is the home of Jim Lane and Jennison; remember that in hunting us they gave no quarter. Shoot every soldier you see, but in no way harm a woman or a child."
>
> He dashed ahead of his command down Main [Massachusetts] Street, firing his pistol twice, dismounted from his horse and went into the hotel [City Hotel], where he was met by the landlord, whom he recognized as an old friend and immediately gave orders for the landlord not to be molested and stayed in the hotel and guarded him.
>
> During all this time, his command were busy hunting men with blue clothes and setting fire to the town. Jim Lane and Jennison were the ones wanted, and some of the boys dashed at once to Jim Lane's house, but, unfortunately for the world, did not find him. They found his saber, which was very handsome, the scabbard being heavily gold-plated. In the parlor of Lane's House there were three pianos and the boys recognized two of them as having belonged to Southern people in Jackson County, and a great many other things belonging to Southern people were found in his house.[23]

Historian Paul Peterson continues in the description of the events that transpired in Lawrence on August 21, 1863:

> The hunted men were soldiers, militiamen, Jayhawkers, and Redlegs as well as individuals who had aided jayhawkers, notably individuals who had trafficked in the property stolen from Missourians. Also included were newspapermen who for years had expounded virulent, caustic and inflammatory articles. No small example of this was John Speer Sr. He had once written of the guerrillas: "Of all the mean, miserable creatures that infest the Earth, these canine wretches in human form are the most despicable."
>
> Quantrill's men carried maps that noted the houses marked for destruction. Once a house had been put to the torch, guerrillas surrounded it to ensure the flames were not extinguished and that the house was completely destroyed. . . .
>
> Any house with porch steps made from gravestones stolen from Missouri cemeteries, as well as any house where any property was recognized as stolen from Missouri, raised the guerrillas' wrath and indignation. They felt compelled to use the torch freely in such instances..
>
> Three hundred buildings comprised the town; the guerrillas singled out around 40 for destruction, mostly in the commercial district that housed or made their business by dealing in plundered goods. Because other buildings caught fire and suffered collateral damage due to their proximity to the condemned buildings, more than 80 buildings were eventually destroyed in the flames. . . .

Contrary to what others have written, Quantrill ordered the bloodshed at Lawrence to be minimal. The refugee Savage noted: "It would have been much worse for Lawrence if Quantrill had not been along." John Newman Edwards added: "Quantrill, during the entire occupation, did not fire his pistol. He saw everything, directed everything, was the one iron man, watchful and vigilant through everything; but he did not kill. He saved many."

Years after the war, an article from *The Cincinnati Enquirer,* reprinted in the April 22, 1898 *Topeka Mail and Breeze*, asserted:

> As a matter of fact, investigation has shown that Quantrill's methods of warfare were not looked upon with favor by some. He was too humane, and generally shrank from the needless taking of human life. He led the 300 guerrillas against Lawrence, Kansas, and helped sack the town of Olathe, but those living today, who were under his command on those memorable occasions, have testified that Quantrill's horror of needless blood-spilling held his men very much in check and minimized the slaughter.[24]

Quantrill & Jesse James

The conflict in the Missouri/Kansas border area was brutal. Many of the young men of the region were hardened in the forge of battle—their brothers and fathers participating in the skirmishes and raids to protect personal property and avenge murders and thefts. Several famous young fast guns were brought up in this maelstrom. One of them was Jesse James. Here is a young Jesse, about the time he was a Confederate guerrilla with William Quantrill. He is said to have joined when he was 15. This picture purports to show Jesse at age 17. James would later become the most famous American outlaw, successfully robbing trains and banks for 15 years until he was (allegedly) killed by a member of his own gang in 1882. Also riding with Quantrill were Frank James and the Younger brothers—Cole, Jim and Bob. These men were rough Rebel guerrillas; tough fighters, expert marksmen and horsemen, able to live off the land. No surprise it took so long to put these boys out of commission once they started turning their guerrilla skills to robbing banks, trains and stagecoaches.

WOMEN AND CHILDREN NOT HARMED

Even the *Lawrence* [Kansas] *Journal-World* newspaper, in its Sunday, September 19, 2004 edition, which republished an account first printed in 1929, admitted that women and children were not harmed by Confederate Partisans in the raid on Lawrence, stating that:

> The invaders divided into parties of six or eight and seemed to infest the whole town. Men, wherever found, were shot down and their homes set afire. Women and children were not harmed, but women's pleas were disregarded.[25]

Quantrill and his Missouri Partisans, unlike Lane and his Jayhawkers, did not burn or loot Lawrence for envy of the town's prosperity, for it is fact that Lawrence prospered through the theft of Missourians' property which was earned through ingenuity and hard work. They did not possess a "moral high ground" of a thinly disguised mission of saving one society through the destruction of another.

The reasons for Quantrill's actions, and the Missourians who rode with him, can be summed up in the battle cries heard as they galloped into Lawrence: "Remember Osceola. Remember the Girls!" ❖

ENDNOTES:

[1]*Battle Cry of Freedom*, McPherson, 786.

[2]*Quantrill of Missouri*, Peterson, 57-8.

[3]Missouri Partisan Ranger website, Missouri Partisan Act: www.rulen.com/partisan/part_act.htm.

[4]*Quantrill of Missouri*, 61.

[5]*Ibid.*, 61-3.

[6]*Ibid.*

[7]*Ibid.*

[8]*Civil War on the Western Border*, Monaghan, 197.

[9]*Ibid.*

[10]*Civil War on the Western Border*, Monaghan, 196.

[11]*The Writings of Abraham Lincoln*, Vol. V, found at the following internet address: www.fullbooks.com/The-Writings-of-Abraham-Lincoln-v55.html.

[12]*Bushwhackers of the Border*, Brophy, 47.

[13]*Ibid.*, 46.

[14]"Quantrill: Soldier or Murderer," Kelley, article found at the following internet address: www.americanhistory.about.com.

[15]*Inside War*, Fellman, 254.

[16]*The Hard Hand of War*, Grimsley, 51.

[17]*Quantrill of Missouri*, 241.

[18]*Ibid.*, 247.

[19]Collapse of Union Jail in Kansas City, Missouri Partisan Ranger website found at the following internet address: www.rulen.com/partisan/collapse.htm.

[20] *Quantrill of Missouri*, 251-2.

[21] *Ibid.*, 252-3.

[22] *Three Years With Quantrill*, Barton, 122-3.

[23] *Ibid.*, 124-6.

[24] *Quantrill of Missouri*, 294-9.

[25] "Quantrill's raid left Lawrence in ruins, killed 143 men," from the September 19, 2004 edition of *The Lawrence World-Journal* newspaper.

Clint E. Lacy is a historian with the John T. Coffee Camp 1934, Missouri Sons of Confederate Veterans. His has written several other fine articles for The Barnes Review including: "Confederate Flag" (Sept./Oct. 2005) and "The Wilson Massacre" (Jan./Feb. 2007).

NOTE: This article first appeared in the November/December 2007 issue of the bimonthly historical journal The Barnes Review. TBR is $46 for one year. Call 1-877-773-9077 toll free to order or visit www.barnesreview.com.

John Wesley Hardin: Fugitive from Injustice

Who was John Wesley Hardin? Was he the greatest "shootist" of the Old West? And why has he been vilified, blackballed and slighted?

By Gary Lee Yarbrough

If one were to ask the average American to name a few of the most notorious Old West gunfighters, most would come up with "Wild Bill" Hickok, Wyatt Earp or Billy the "Kid." Occasionally one might hear Clay Allison, "Doc" Holliday or even Johnny Ringo. Rarely, however, would John Wesley "Little Arkansas" Hardin, the deadliest and most successful gunfighter of them all, be mentioned.

The reason Wes Hardin's name is unfamiliar to most of us today is because Wes was unabashedly politically incorrect. The spin-doctors, therefore, relegated Wes to the Orwellian "memory hole" and opted to extol other less qualified characters as the preeminent gunfighters of Old West fame (notably Hickok and Earp) many of whom have figured prominently in movies or had entire TV series devoted to them. Hardin, or a mythological version of the real-life man (often with new myths added), has appeared briefly in several movies and TV shows, and was sung about by Bob Dylan (under the name of Harding).

Also a small, independent movie was produced in 1974 called "John Wesley Hardin—A Western," starring Mike Baccaro, produced and directed by Frank Jolley. This was later re-edited as "The Young'un—A Story of John Wesley Hardin" and appeared in the Independent Feature Film Market at the Angelica Theater in New York City. It is available on the Internet.

But otherwise John Wesley Hardin has received little media play.

James Butler Hickok, aka "Wild Bill," in reliable, published accounts, is credited with no more than 15 kills. Of that number, more than a few were of unarmed men. In fact the first three men Hickok killed were all unarmed. The first man was shot and killed through a curtain partition because Hickok was terrified to face him. He had tormented Hickok for months about his feminine features and called Hickok a hermaphrodite on numerous occasions.

While more famous gunfighters, like "Wild Bill" Hickok get the headlines, it was John Wesley Hardin, shown above, who was actually the most dangerous gun in the Old West. Hickok, for instance, was credited with killing 15 men, more than one of them unarmed. By the time Hardin was 25, it was claimed he had killed 42 men. Almost half of those were heavily armed federal agents, bounty hunters and law officers sent to bring him in.

Wyatt Earp killed less than 10 men. Contrary to Hollywood's version of the Wyatt Earp saga, there is only one body in Dodge City's Boothill Cemetery that is attributed to Wyatt Earp's six-gun. Earp was a con man and horse thief, running a protection racket in the town where he was sheriff. There was evidence to suggest that the Earps and Doc Holliday were the actual stagecoach robbers in Tombstone, Arizona. Earp was convicted of claim-jumping in Eagle City, Idaho in 1880 and later arrested in Los Angeles for fleecing J.Y. Patterson out of $25,000 in a bunko scam.

The total body count of Hickok, Earp and Billy the Kid combined does not top John Wesley Hardin's confirmed 42 kills. Contrary to the historical claim that "John Wesley Hardin was so mean, he once shot a man just for snoring," Hardin stated, "I never killed a man wantonly or in cold blood." Neither Hickok nor Earp could make that claim. In defense of this accusation Wes Hardin warned, "It is never wise to accept the word of a stranger or the newspapers."

John Wesley Hardin was a rebel with a cause and a valiant defender of the South. The second son of James G. Hardin, a teacher and circuit riding Methodist preacher, John's mother, Elizabeth, was also a teacher. And yet his detractors claim that Wes Hardin was illiterate. This is highly unlikely.

John Wesley was born on May 26, 1853, in Bonham, Fannin Co., Texas and named after the founder of the Methodist Church. His grandfather, Benjamin Hardin, was a member of the Texas Congress before the first Union. John Wesley's great uncle, Augustine Hardin, was a signer of the Texas Declaration of Independence. Hardin County, Texas is named after another great uncle, Judge William Hardin. The Hardin family was as big as Texas and prominent in Texan history.

Wes Hardin's first brush with the law came when he was only 14. A schoolhouse bully by the name of Charles Slotter had sullied the name of a girl Wes was sweet on, by writing disparaging remarks about her on the wall of the outhouse and blaming Wes for the deed. When Wes confronted the culprit, a fight ensued. The bully was severely stabbed with a knife. Wes was arrested, charged, tried and acquitted of this incident. The judge and jury praised Wes and claimed the bully got what he had coming to him.

In contrast to Hardin, who respected women, Hickok once kicked a woman in the face because she jilted him. Phil Coe, a Texan who witnessed the deed, soundly beat Hickok to a pulp and was later murdered by Hickok in the streets of Abilene.

Wes Hardin killed his first man at the age of fifteen. A huge ex-slave named Mage touted that he could whip any two white men in a wrestling match. When beaten by Joe and Wes Hardin, Mage became vengeful and stated he would kill Wes when he saw him again; Wes went home and armed himself. On the following day Mage confronted Wes on the road. Mage was carrying a club and tried to pull

Wes from his horse. When the horse shied and reared, Wes shot Mage twice. Incredibly, the huge black man continued to grab for Wes. Four shots later Mage still did not go down, but Wes was able to ride away and return with help for the injured assailant. Mage survived for two days and claimed that Wes was a liar and had murdered him.

This incident of November 1868 was during the Reconstruction Era following the Civil War. For a white man to be tried anywhere in the South for the death of a black man meant certain conviction to prison or hanging. Wes Hardin understood the reality, stating:

> All the courts were then conducted by bureau agents and renegades who were the inveterate enemies of the South and administered a code of justice to suit every case in gross injustice to Southern people. To be tried at that time for killing a Negro meant certain death at the hands of a court backed by Northern bayonets. Thus, willingly, I became a fugitive, not from justice, be it known, but from injustice and misrule of the people who had subjugated the South.

Hardin 's father had this to say in a letter to one Charles Morgan, "Not until the courts of Texas are again halls of true and impartial justice will I encourage my son to stand himself before their judgment." Thus began John Wesley Hardin's career as an outlaw and gunfighter. By Wes Hardin's reasoning, if the Yankees' rule was to be the law in Texas, then his only choice was to be an outlaw.

Texas was occupied by Union soldiers and the State Police appointed by Governor Edmund Davis, himself an appointee of the Northern aggressors. The State Police was composed of carpetbaggers and scalawags from the North: half the force consisted of freed Negroes. According to Wes: "Instead of protecting life, liberty and property, they frequently destroyed it." Wes made a vow to never be taken at the point of a gun.

After the death of Mage, a posse of three Union soldiers spotted Wes and gave chase. Wes outran them and set up a hasty ambush. When the soldiers entered the trap, Wes killed two of them point blank with a shotgun; the third, a Negro, fled on horseback. Wes chased him and jokingly demanded, "Halt, in the name of the Confederacy." The Negro snapped a shot at Wes and then Wes shot him for his effort.

John Wesley Hardin had no respect for and gave no quarter to anyone seeking his arrest. Of the 42 confirmed kills attributed to Wes, more than half served in a law enforcement capacity: soldiers, posse members, state police, Texas Rangers and Pinkerton detectives. Seven of these were Negroes. Wes killed two other Negroes, a rapist and a rioter, two Indians and seven Mexican banditos. Five of the Mexicans he killed at one time, on horseback, in a charge that Quantrill's Raiders

FAST GUNS OF THE WILD WEST

Above are pictured four of the most infamous gunslingers in American history. Left to right above: Wyatt Earp, Doc Holliday, Bat Masterson and Wild Bill Hickok. **Earp**, before becoming marshal of Tombstone, Arizona, was a part-time lawman, maintenance worker and vagrant in Wichita, Kansas. It was in the lawless Dodge City that Earp, Holliday and Masterson met, Masterson being a deputy there along with Earp. **Holliday** occasionally hung out the apothecary sign, but was mostly a gambler and professional card dealer with a bad temper. **Masterson** was a renowned hunter, hired to shoot buffalo—tens of thousands of them. He is reputed to have been an amazingly accurate shot with pistol or rifle and survived the Indian siege of 'Dobe Walls. While hiding behind a curtain, **William Hickok**, far right, shot a man because the man had teased Hickok about his feminine features. While the movies and museums may be dedicated to this collection of "dead eyes," John Wesley Hardin surpassed them all for real, man-to-man gunfighting.

would have envied.

Following the deaths of Mage and the three-man posse, Wes Hardin tried to avoid any more bloodshed and went to live with relatives in Navarro Co., Texas. There he taught school until he was informed that the authorities were notified of his whereabouts. Again, seeking to avoid trouble and his arrest, Wes joined friends on a cattle drive up the Chisholm Trail to its northern most point, Abilene, Kansas, where the marshal was none other than the legendary Wild Bill Hickok.

Hickok was widely known for hatred and mistreatment of Texans. However, Wes intended to make his acquaintance. News of Hardin's arrival preceded him up the Chisholm Trail. It was on this drive that Wes killed the five Mexicans at the Arkansas River crossing. Word of this incident worried Hickok, as it takes a bit of skill to kill five men in open, armed combat. When the two gunfighters eventually crossed paths in an Abilene saloon Hardin tried to goad Hickok into a gun fight by telling him that he heard that Wild Bill was a "Texan-hating Yankee son-of-a-bitch" and that the world would be better off without him, adding that Wild Bill "preferred killing Texans to Mexicans and niggers."

Hickok, aware of Hardin's intent, responded saying, "Folks will believe what they want to believe," and offered to buy Hardin a drink.

The ordinance banning the wearing of firearms within city limits was not strictly enforced. The law was applied arbitrarily as a means to levy and collect fines from people who could be intimidated into doing so. Over a few left-handed drinks Bill and Wes became friendly toward one another—as much as two gunslingers could be friends anyway.

Hardin's cousin Joe Clements had been arrested by one of Hickok's deputies and Wes asked Hickok to release him. Hickok said he would. Before retiring for the evening, Hickok asked Wes to help keep the rowdy Texas cattle hands in line while they were in Abilene; to this Wes agreed. But when Hickok said, "You might also do me a favor by not wearing them guns in town," Hardin turned and walked away.

The following day while making his rounds, Hickok approached the Bull's Head Saloon, the Texans' favorite hangout. Hickok noticed a cowboy amble inside. A moment later Hardin walked out, dressed to the nines and packing twin .44-caliber Colts on his hips. The windows and doors of the saloon immediately filled with grinning Texan faces. Hickok, also dressed to the nines, hailed Hardin a little distance from the saloon. "I thought we had an understanding about them pistols, 'Little Arkansas'?" ("Little Arkansas" was a nickname given to Wes after he killed the five Mexicans at the river crossing.)

Hickok's deputy moved behind Wes, leveling a double-barrel shotgun at Wes's back. Hardin remarked that he was on his way out of town. Appeased, Hickok turned to leave.

A loud "rebel yell" erupted from the Bull's Head Saloon. Startled, Hickok swung around and pulled a Navy Colt. Hardin, distracted by the yell also, looked back at Hickok to find himself looking into the barrel of a gun. Hickok told Hardin to hand over his guns butt first. Wes drew his guns and held them out butt first, but placed his index fingers in both trigger guards and rolled and cocked his pistols in a flash and stuck them in Hickok's face. A roar of cheers came from the Bull's Head patrons, as Hardin told Hickok to drop the Navy Colt. Naturally, Hickok refused. The two gunfighters were in a Mexican standoff. Hickok told Hardin to holster his guns and leave town. Wes told Hickok he was not going to allow Hickok to shoot him in the back. Hickok put his gun away.

The Texans yelled for Hardin to "kill the son-of-a-bitch." But Hardin holstered his guns and calmly walked away. This occurred in November 1871 when John Wesley Hardin was only 18 years old. Hickok would later become an alcoholic and opium addict, going blind from gonorrhea.

In August of 1872 Wes Hardin killed a police officer and wounded another after an attempt to arrest Wes for the reward money offered on him. One year later, Sheriff Charles Webb tried to back shoot Wes after offering to buy Wes a drink. When Wes turned to enter the saloon, Webb pulled his gun and fired one round, which grazed Hardin's ribs. Hardin spun and killed Webb.

The decade of the 1870s was a time of great turbulence and violence in the Southwest and especially in Texas. Under Reconstruction law, Yankee, Negro and mob rule plagued the land. John Wesley and friends openly opposed black, mob rule and tyranny in general. Wes later wrote, "In putting down Negro rule in Gonzales I made many friends, and made it a thing of the past for a Negro to hold office in that county." Jack Helms was sheriff of DeWitt and Gonzales counties in 1873. He was, also, a captain of a vigilante mob. Before killing Helms, Wes told him: "You have made life, liberty and property uncertain. You have been killing men long enough. I know you belong to a legalized band of murdering cowards, and have hanged and murdered better men than yourself."

Eventually a mob took Hardin's family and relatives hostage, including his wife, Jane, and newborn daughter, Molly, forcing Wes to leave Texas. He fled to Florida, where he was later reunited with Jane, who gave birth to their second child, John W. Hardin Jr.

In 1874 Hardin's brother Joe, a lawyer, was lynched by a mob. Their parents and his younger brother, Jefferson Davis Hardin, moved to Navarro County, Texas. Wes was eventually captured in Florida in 1878, 10 years after the killing of Mage. He was extradited to Gonzales, Texas, to stand trial for killing the back-shooting sheriff, Charles Webb. At that time in Texas a man accused of murder could not testify on his own behalf. Hardin's witnesses were either dead or wanted themselves by the authorities. The best defense Wes had was a witness for the prosecution who testified that Webb had fired first, then fired again just as Hardin's bullet struck him. It was not known if Wes had actually killed Webb, since others had riddled Webb with bullets as he fell to the boardwalk.

The presiding judge was prejudiced because John's older brother Joe had beaten him in a land dispute years before. Five of the jurors were participants in the mob lynching of Joe Hardin. Wes was sentenced to 25 years in prison; he was 26 years old.

In the Texas State Prison at Huntsville John Wesley read constantly. Between escape attempts, bull-whippings and isolation, Wes studied algebra, geometry, history and theology. Since prison informants and a ball and chain made it impossible to escape, Wes became a model prisoner. He was superintendent of Sunday school and president of the debating society. Wes became interested in and studied law.

After 15 years, nine months and 12 days John Wesley Hardin was pardoned. He passed the Texas State Bar exam and opened a law office in El Paso, Texas. His devoted wife died one year prior to his release from prison.

Wes was murdered on August 19, 1895, by Sheriff John Selman, who walked into the Acme Saloon and shot Wes in the back of the head as he was rolling dice. Selman was charged with murder but was acquitted and he resumed his duties as an officer of the law. Several months later Selman was killed in a gunfight with a United States deputy marshal.

John Wesley Hardin's record and character must not be blackballed and slighted in truth. He was a just and honest man in an unjust and corrupted land. Though Hardin was an outlaw rebel, he never stole a penny in his life, nor wronged anyone who was not trying to wrong him. It is not difficult to understand why Hardin's true-life story is suppressed, however, nor why Hickok and Earp's stories have been romanticized and exaggerated. Both were Northerners from Illinois. Both were loyal to the Union and both were officers of the "law," which was corrupt and unjust. The truth is, the North must have been hard-pressed for heroes to glorify these two contemptible wretches.

John Wesley Hardin was the king of pistoleros, a true hero. In his own words: "I was always a child of nature, her ways and moods were my study. The man who does not exercise the first law of nature—that of self-preservation—is not worthy of living and breathing the breath of life." ❖

BIBLIOGRAPHY:

Blake, James Carlos, *The Pistoleer*, 1996.
Braun, Matt, *Noble Outlaw*, Wheeler Large Print Book Series, 1996.
Jackson, Jack, Lost Cause: *John Wesley Hardin, the Taylor-Sutton Feud, and Reconstruction in Texas*, 1998.
McGinnis, Bruce, *Reflections in Dark Glass: The Life and Times of John Wesley Hardin*, 1996.
Metz, Leon Claire, *John Wesley Hardin: Dark Angel of Texas*, 1998.
Miller, Rick, *Bounty Hunter*, 1988.
Parsons, Chuck, *The Capture of John Wesley Hardin* (The Young West series), 1978.
Patterson, C.L., *Sensational Texas Manhunt*, 1939.
Plenn, Jaime Harrysson, *The Fastest Gun in Texas*, 1990.
Ripley, Thomas, *They Died With Their Boots On*, 1937.
Sonnichsen, C.L., *The Grave of John Wesley Hardin* (Essays on the American West, No. 5), 1980.
Stamps, Roy and Jo Ann Stamps, *The Letters of John Wesley Hardin*, 2001.

NOTE: This article first appeared in the May/June 2007 issue of the bimonthly historical journal THE BARNES REVIEW. TBR is $46 for one year. Call 1-877-773-9077 toll free to order or visit www.barnesreview.com.

GARY LEE YARBROUGH is a member of the Bruders Schweigen, or the "Order." Yarbrough married a girl from the Hardin clan. Convicted of burglary and accused of shooting at federal agents who attacked the Order's headquarters, he was incarcerated. While in prison he was brutally assaulted and crippled by federal guards.

And If Hitler Had Won?

"ALTERNATIVE HISTORY" (also called allohistory, counterfactual history or uchronia) is the description or discussion of a historical "what if," with speculation about the consequences of a different event than what really happened. Here, Leon Degrelle looks at the fascinating question of "What would our world today be like if the Nazis had won World War II?" What if Adolf Hitler had won World War II? That is a big question.

BY LÉON DEGRELLE

Let us suppose Germany had won World War II. For a long time, such an eventuality seemed quite possible. In October 1941, Hitler was close to conquering Moscow (he had reached the outskirts of it) and controlling the Volga River from its source northwest of Moscow, having reached it, down to its mouth, of which he was within range. Moscow was waiting only for the appearance of the Reich's tanks on Red Square to rebel. Josef Stalin would have fled. It would have been over. Some German columns of occupation, following the example of Adm. Aleksandr Kolchak in 1919, would have quickly traversed Siberia, or been parachuted there. At the edge of the Pacific Ocean, the swastika flag would have waved above Vladivostok, 6,000 miles from the Rhine.

What would the reactions of the world have been? England at the end of 1941 might have lain down its arms at any time. One evening of too much whiskey would have sufficed for Winston Churchill to crumple into an armchair, drooling, felled by a stroke. That this inveterate boozer was able to preserve himself in alcohol for so long is a case for the doctors to study for years. His personal physician, anyway, has published since his death some very comical details of the Bacchic endurance of his famous patient.

But even living, Churchill was dependent on the mood of his public. In 1941 the English public was still trying to bear up—but it was tired. The conquest of

Russia by Hitler, freeing up the whole Luftwaffe, would have succeeded in crushing them. This war—what was it leading to? Moreover, what had it led to? In 1945 England finished the war totally naked, as Hitler had predicted, deprived of her whole empire, and brought in the eyes of the world to the status of a secondary state at the end of her years of striptease. A Chamberlain, instead of a Churchill, would long before have raised a white flag on the tip of his umbrella.[1]

Confronting alone a victorious Germany—whose empire, without equal in the world and gorged with all its resources, spread over 7,000 miles wide, from the Anglo- Norman islands in the North Sea to Sakhalin Island in the Pacific—England would have been no better than a lifeboat whirling in a cyclone. She could not have resisted the waves for long. Churchill would have gotten tired—and the English before him—of emptying endless buckets of water from a more and more overwhelmed vessel.

Take refuge farther away? In Canada? (Churchill, flask on his hip, might have become a trapper or restaurateur there, but not a savior.) In Africa, perhaps? Or the East Indies? The British empire was already lost. It could not serve as the last springboard of a resistance that no longer made sense.[2]

No one would even have spoken anymore of Charles de Gaulle, who would have become a professor in Ottawa, rereading Saint-Simon in the evening or holding between his hands a skein of wool for his diligent Aunt Yvonne to knit.[3]

A STROKE OF LUCK

The English victory was really the stroke of luck of a stubborn old man running on alcohol, lashed bewildered to a split mast and hearing sinister cracking sounds, to whom the gods of the drunkards had been exceptionally indulgent.[4]

Never mind. Once the USSR was in Hitler's hands, in the autumn of 1941, the flames of English resistance would have sputtered out, with or without Churchill.

As for the Americans, they had not yet entered the war at this time [fall of 1941]. Japan was observing them, preparing to pounce. Once Europe was his, Hitler would no more have gotten involved with Japan than Japan, in June 1941, would have interfered in the German offensive against the USSR.

The United States, kept busy in Asia for a long time, would not have saddled itself with another war in Europe. The military conflict between Hitler and the United States would not have taken place, in spite of the warmongering itches of old Roosevelt, turned green and cadaver-like in his coachman's cape, in spite of the incitement of his wife Eleanor—all her teeth on display, sticking out like the spines on a caterpillar.

Let us say, then, that at the end of autumn 1941—it would have taken him just 15 minutes by Moscow streetcar—Hitler had installed himself in the Kremlin, just as he had entered the palaces of Vienna in 1938, of Prague in 1939, and the armistice coach of Compiègne in 1940.

What would have happened in Europe?

Hitler would undoubtedly have unified Europe, by force.

All great deeds in the world are done by force. This is regrettable, you will say. It would certainly be more proper for the worthy citizens, the patronesses of the church parish, and the fearless vestal virgins of the Salvation Army to gather us democratically together in peaceful territorial units, smelling of chocolate, mimosa and holy water. But it never happens like that. The Capetian dynasty did not carve out the kingdom of France through elections with universal suffrage.[5]

One province after another of it was dropped into the royal bed, at the same time as Hugh Capet's nightshirt, by a young, wiggling wife. [Adele or Adelaide of Aquitaine was about 18 or 25 when they married; Hugh ruled only over a small patch of land from about Paris to Orleans; there was no "France" as we know it in those days.—Ed.] The rest of French territory was gradually stolen over the centuries, by means of the sword.

In the north, conquered by the royal armies, the inhabitants were chased out of their cities—notably Arras—like rats. In the south, in the "Albigensian" resistance to Louis VIII [1209-1229], the Cathars, beaten, burned and crucified by the crusaders of the crown, were roasted in their fortress-castles, sort of pre-Hitlerian crematories.[6]

The Protestants of Adm. Gaspard Coligny found themselves at the end of the pikes of the Saint-Bartholomew's Day Massacre or swinging from the ropes of the gibbet of Montfaucon.[7]

The revolution of the Marats [as in Jean-Paul Marat] and the Fouquier-Tinvilles [as in Antoine Quentin Fouquier-Tinville] preferred to assert authority through the shiny steel of the guillotine and its basket of straw, rather than through glassfuls of red wine offered to voters at the corner café.[8]

NAILED DOWN

Even Napoleon nailed down the borders of his empire with a bayonet. Catholic Spain did not invite the occupying Moors, to the rhythm of castanets, to become good Spaniards. It ripped their guts out enthusiastically for all the seven centuries of the *Reconquista* until the last of the Muslim invaders ran for his life back to the palm trees on the shores of North Africa. The Arabs had been no friendlier either, when they united the south of Spain for their own profit—nailing resistant Spaniards to the gates of their own cities, as for example in Cordoba—crucified between a dog and pig, both protesting vociferously.

During the last century, Bismarck forged German unity with cannon at Sadowa and Sedan. Garibaldi did not pull together the Italian states with a rosary in his hand, but by organizing an assault on pontifical Rome. The American states themselves did not become united until after the elimination of their former owners, the "redskins," and after four long years of very un-democratic slaughter during the War of Dixie's Secession.

Only the Swiss founded more or less peacefully their little state of café-owners, archers, maidservants and milkmen. But, except for the burst apple of William Tell, their worthy cantons hardly shone in the history of universal politics.

Have all the big empires and the big countries been created by force?

Maybe it is regrettable, but it is a fact.

Hitler, encamped in a stubborn Europe, would certainly have behaved no worse than Caesar conquering Gaul, than Louis XIV seizing Artois and the Roussillon, than the English conquering the Irish, robbing and persecuting them, or than the Americans aiming the cannon of their cruisers on the Philippines, on Puerto Rico, on Cuba and on Panama, or extending their military borders by rocket blasts to the 37th Vietnamese parallel.

Democracy, that is to say the electoral consent of the people, does not come until afterward, once the conquest is over.

The masses see the universe through the keyhole of their small personal preoccupations. Never would a Breton, a Fleming or a Catalan of the Roussillon, of their own volition, have worked to put together a united France. The people of Baden stubbornly remain Badensers, the people of Wuerttemberg, Wuerttembergers. The father of one of my Hamburg friends expatriated himself to the United States after 1870 rather than see himself integrated into the empire of William I.

It is the elites who create the world. And it is the strong who, boots to backsides, push the weak forward. Without them the peoples, fragmented, would never get anywhere.

In 1941 or in 1942, even if Hitler's victory in Europe had been total and irreversible, even if, as our Belgian eternal cabinet minister [Paul-Henri] Spaak [who also served as prime minister] has said, Germany was going to be "the mistress of Europe for a thousand years," the grousers would have multiplied by the millions. Each would have clung to his habits and to his own corner of the country—which was superior, obviously, to all other corners of the country. As a student I always listened with stupefaction to my friends of Charleroi screaming over their cases of beer: *Land of Charleroi/It's you that I prefer./The most beautiful place on the Earth/Yes, 'tis you, yes, 'tis you.*

Well, Charleroi is the ugliest place on the face of the Earth, with its interminable mining villages built of blackish brick, beneath hundreds of towers of dusty slagheaps. Even the flowers there are sprinkled with coal dust. Yet, eyes shining, these Charleroian buddies brayed their enthusiasm. Each person is infatuated with his village, his region, his kingdom, his republic.[9]

NAPOLEON'S DREAM

But this European complex of the petty and insignificant could evolve, and was even in the process of evolving. An accelerated evolution would have been anything but impracticable. It had been proven 10 times over, that it was possible to unite Europeans who are very distant from each other and yet are fundamentally the same.

The 100,000 French Protestants who had to leave their country after the revocation of the Edict of Nantes amalgamated marvelously with the Prussians who took them in. During our campaign of February and March 1945, in the villages east and west of the Oder, we saw everywhere, on the nameplates of peasants' carts distinguished French names savoring of the soil of Anjou and Aquitaine.

On the front lines German-French names like von Dieu le Veut, von Mezières, von de la Chevalerie etc abounded.[10]

The Napoleonic empire, too, gathered Europeans together without asking their advice. Yet, it was fascinating how remarkably quickly their elites joined together: the German Goethe became a knight of the *Legion d'honneur,* the Polish prince Poniatowski became marshal of France; Goya provided Spanish masterpieces to the Louvre Museum; Napoleon proclaimed himself, on his coins, *Rex Italicus.*

The soldiers of Napoleon's Old Guard, recruited in 10 different European countries, rubbed elbows with one another, fraternizing exactly as we would in our turn in the ranks of the Waffen SS during World War II. But each time, to start the process required either persecution, or war, or the necessity to earn one's bread, or the willpower of a strongman. Something had to drive us together.

Normally the peoples of Europe each kept to the security of their own borders. That did not prevent some from occasionally pushing the boundaries, however—and each time with success.

These fecund experiences, occurring in stages over time, had already united the most diverse Europeans—Prussians from north Germany with Aquitainians from southern France, men of Flanders with southern Spaniards in Andalusia or with Sicilians, could very well happen again, and in greater measure.[11]

Won or lost, WWII would provide a strong impetus. It had forced all Europeans—and notably the adversaries who appeared the most irreconcilable, the French and the Germans—to associate with one another, even if they hated one another; even if they dreamed of nothing but kicking one another in the shins.

Who Was Leon Degrelle?

In its quest to produce a definitive record of missing aspects of history, The Barnes Review magazine commissioned the last wartime German National Socialist leader who was, at the time, still alive and free to fill the gap. This man was Leon Degrelle, the Catholic leader of the Belgian Rexist movement and wartime leader of the Waffen SS volunteer legion "Wallonie."

Degrelle knew Adolf Hitler intimately and was one of his trusted colleagues. He was also acquainted with Churchill, Mussolini and every other major figure of WWII. He was a Belgian (speaking and writing in French as his mother tongue). Along with most other people of Belgium, he was brought up in an anti-German atmosphere.

In the years before the outbreak of war, Degrelle was a young intellectual who published a daily newspaper and organized a national political party that sent representatives to the Belgian parliament. The popular enthusiasm he generated was reflected in the turnout of millions who applauded his message and supported his program.

Degrelle published more than 40 books and essays, ranging from poetry to economics, from architecture to history. He has been acknowledged as a passionate orator and a soldier of rare valor.

Recognizing that Hitler's Germany was Europe's only hope to survive the horrors of Boshevism, Degrelle joined the ranks of the 600,000 foreign volunteers of the Waffen SS as a private and gained the rank of colonel at the front. After four continuous years in the inferno of battle, his legion was one of the last to retreat from Russia. This titanic struggle is described in his famous epic, *Campaign in Russia*, which earned him renown as the "Homer of the 20th century." After the warm Francisco Franco gave him asylum and promoted him to the rank of general. One of the most highly decorated heroes of the deadly eastern front, he was uniquely qualified to observe history objectively. In Belgium today, thanks to a special anti-free-speech law passed for the purpose, it is illegal to transfer, possess or receive any book by or about Degrelle.

—Willis A. Carto

These four years of beating one another up or getting along, of needing to try to understand one another and figure the other out—because they had to—would not be in vain. They had to confront each other face-to-face, winners and losers. Neither would forget the personality of the other. The bad moments would blur. They would remember, then, only what counted. The *rapprochement* of the European peoples had been accomplished.[12]

EUROPE IS ONE

During the 25 years that followed this encounter, other meetings took place to the cadence, and at the speed, of our time. Tens of millions of Europeans travel now. The foreigner is no longer a creature to be observed with fear or hatred or mocked. One chats with him. The Frenchman from Bresse no longer peers at the universe solely over the edge of his blue cheeses and his gold-banded, blue-legged Bresse hens. The Norman has surpassed his cider press, and the Belgian his tart, bubbly beer. Thousands of Swedes live on the coast of Màlaga.[13]

The French tire family Michelin allied with the Italian car family of Agnelli, and the German billionaire Gunther Sachs was able to marry, without triggering the collapse of the republic, a "made in Paris" actress.

Even Gen. Charles de Gaulle thought it not in bad taste to reveal to the French that he had German blood in his veins.

The young often do not even have a country anymore. They feel denationalized. They have created for themselves their own world: a world of audacious or quirky ideas, of frenetic music and lanky hair, of tattered pants, of gaudy shirts and of girls who are largely open to the mixing of nationalities.

The French rooster of 1914 and the black German eagle hovering over the city have stopped cock-a-doodle-do'ing and screaming. Their feathers, beaks and hovering appear already, to the new generation, like strange prehistoric exhibits for museums that will not even be visited.[14]

GLOBAL CLOSENESS

This European, and even world closeness, which has outstripped all the centuries of the past in a quarter of a century, is occurring today without a political stimulus—merely through circulating by the millions from one country to another movie and television images, to be watched by millions, that display other landscapes and other faces.

Customs have mingled as naturally as the different ingredients in a cocktail.

Under Hitler, certainly, the process of unification would have progressed even more quickly, and above all, less anarchically.

A massive common political edifice would have oriented and concentrated all the different tendencies. First, the millions of youths, non-German as well as German, who had fought together from the Vistula to the Volga, had become friends for life in the face of death, through the efforts and sufferings undergone together. They knew each other. They esteemed each other. The petty European rivalries from former times, the remains of bourgeois obsessions, appeared trivial to us.

This "us" was, in 1945, just a core. But in the center of the biggest fruit there is a core, a seed, a principle. We were that core. Europe, a doughy mass, had never had one, but now it existed. It already bore the future.

To all the young, it offered a world to be created, born already of genius and of arms. The millions of young Europeans who had remained low-profile during the war, eating from papa's tin cans and testing the waters of the black market, would be tempted in their turn to do something grand.

Instead of vegetating in Belgian burgs like *Caudebec-en-Caux* or in *Wuustwezel*, living for 50 years on pickled herrings or overripe apples, the millions of enthusiastic youngsters would have seen, spread out before them [by Hitler's conquest of the USSR], the worlds without end of the east, offered to all, whether they were from Frisia in Holland, from Lozère in southern France, from Mecklenburg in eastern Germany or the Abruzzi east of Rome. There it would be possible to carve for themselves a real man's life, as initiators, creators, leaders.

All Europe would have been electrified by this current of energy.

The ideal that had won the hearts of all of the Third Reich's youth in so very few years, because it signified audacity, talent, honor, the yearning for greatness, would have won the heart of the youth of all Europe in exactly the same way. *Finis* their mediocre lives. *Finis,* the endless gray horizons. *Finis,* life glued to the same village, to the same job, to the same apartment in the same mediocre building, to the basket of prejudices of their parents, stuck in their petty and mold-covered lives.

A vibrant world would hail those youth across thousands of kilometers without borders, a world where one could open his lungs wide, have a voracious appetite, swallow great mouthfuls of everything, and conquer great handfuls of everything, in joy and faith.

Even the old would have followed, because in the end money would have followed.

Instead of stagnating in embittered political consultations, with clock timers turned off so that debates could be prolonged, we would have had the iron will of a chief and the decisions of the staffs assigned to create his life's work on a grand scale, who in 20 years would have created a real Europe—not a convention of hesitators gnawed by mistrust and hidden calculations, but a grand political, social and economic unit, with no sector holding back.

You should have heard Hitler, in his wooden field encampment, expounding on his big projects for the future.

Giant canals would unite all the large European rivers, open to the boats of every country, from the Seine to the Volga, from the Vistula to the Danube. Two-story trains, with cargo below and travelers above, on raised tracks 12 feet wide, would comfortably traverse the immense territories of the east, where the soldiers of yesterday would build the agricultural operations of today and the most modern industries in the world.

What are these endlessly discussed "consortiums," limping on their bureaucratic wooden legs, which have been attempted under the aegis of the present Common Market, compared to the great ensembles a real authority could have achieved by uniting European economic strengths that were formerly disparate and contradictory or hostile, selfish and anarchistic, shooting themselves in the feet by duplicating processes that might have been combined? The hand of a master would quickly have brought them back to the law of intelligent co-production and common interest.

For 20 years the public would have grumbled and balked. But by the end of one generation, unity would have been achieved. Europe would have constituted the biggest reservoir of creative intelligence there has ever been. The European masses could have breathed then. The discipline could have been relaxed once this battle for Europe had been won.[15]

WOULD GERMANY HAVE DEVOURED EUROPE?

Would Germany have devoured Europe?

The danger existed. Why deny it? The same danger had existed previously: Napoleon's France could have devoured Europe. But personally, I do not believe it. The genius of each European nation would have offset the other.

The same appetite for domination would undoubtedly have tempted a Hitlerian Europe. Germans are big eaters. Some considered Europe as their own banquet. They were capable of acts of sabotage, of trickery. Oh yes, oh yes. We realized it. We feared it. If we had not, we would have been simpletons, or at least naïve, which in politics is no better. We took precautions, attempting to seize as firmly as possible positions of control or prestige from which we could defend ourselves, raise a fuss or cut off finances.

There were risks; that is very true. To deny the fact would be imbecilic. But there were also reasons for confidence that were just as strong.

Hitler, first of all, was a man accustomed to see very far, and who was not blinded by German exclusivity. He had been by turns Austrian, then "German," then "Greater-German."[16]

After 1941, he had passed all those stages—he was a "European." Genius rises above frontiers and ethnic lines. Napoleon, too, had at first been solely Corsican, and even an anti-French Corsican.[17]

At the end, on the island of Saint-Helen, he spoke of the "French people whom [he loved] so much" as a valued people, but not exclusively "his."

What does genius want? Always to surpass itself. The larger the mass of human dough he has to knead, the more a genius is in his element. In 1811 Napoleon had already reached the Indies in his mind.

Europe was a project of the appropriate size for Hitler. Germany was no more than an important building that he had built previously, and that he watched with complaisance. But he had already gone much further.

On his part, no real danger existed of a Germanization of Europe. That was the extreme opposite of everything that his ambition, his pride and his genius aimed at and dictated to him.

But weren't there other Germans? Yes, but there were also other Europeans. And these other Europeans possessed their own exceptional qualities, indispensable to the Germans, without which the German-ruled Europe would have been a heavy pastry, badly leavened. I am referring, above all, to the genius of France. The Germans would never have been able to do without the genius of France in order to give life to Europe, although they would rather have not needed recourse to it and, in the case of some Germans, looked down on it.

But nothing was possible, and nothing will ever be possible in Europe without the finesse and grace of the French, without the vivacity and the clarity of the French mind. The French people have the quickest intelligence. The French mind captures, it grasps, it exalts, it transfigures. It is quick. It is light. The French taste for things is perfect. Never will there be a second cupola of the Invalides Hospital. [Built by the "Sun King," Louis XIV, in 1670 as a veterans' home, the Invalides houses the tomb of Napoleon, and was one of the sites Hitler visited, both for the tomb and for the architecture, in May 1940.—Ed.]

Never will there be another valley as charming as the Loire with its castles. Never will there be such chic, such charm, such *joie de vivre* as in Paris.

Hitler's Europe would have been heavy in the beginning. Next to a Goering, a Renaissance nobleman, who had a sense of art and splendor, and a Goebbels with his scalpel-sharp intelligence, a number of Hitlerian leaders were heavy, vulgar as cowherds, tasteless, turning out their doctrine, their ideas and their orders, as if they were producing chopped meat or chemical fertilizer. But precisely because of this heaviness, the French genius would have been indispensable. In 10 years, it would have put its stamp on everything.

ITALIANS AND RUSSIANS

The Italian genius, as well, would have provided a counterweight to the too-solid energy of the Germans.

The Italians are often ridiculed. But since the war we have seen what they are capable of. They would have flooded a Hitlerian Europe with their impeccable shoes, their elegant fashions, their cars as well-bred as greyhounds, as easily as they do the narrow flowerbeds of a young Common Market.[18]

The Russian genius would also have had a hand to a considerable degree, I am sure of it, in refining a too-German Europe, in which 200 million Slavs from the east were going to be integrated. Four years of living mingled with the Russian people caused the German warriors to admire and like them. The misfortune is that, for a half-century, the virtues of these 200 million brave people have been choked—under the enormous leaden bell of the Soviet régime. [Written before the USSR collapsed.—Ed.]

These people, peaceful, sensitive, intelligent and artistic, are also gifted in mathematics—which is not a contradiction, for the laws of numbers constitute the basis of all the arts as well as the sciences.

When we entered Russia, the Germans, who had been subject to a really too perfunctory Nazi indoctrination, imagined that the only worthwhile beings in the universe were their own Aryans, who were required to be blond giants, built like barrel organs, blonder than chamomile tea, eyes blue as a Tyrolean sky in the month of August.

HITLER NOT NORDIC

That's rather funny, since Hitler, although blue of eyes, was not tall, and he had rather dark, chestnut-brown hair.[19] Goebbels had one leg shorter than the other, was short in stature and was as swarthy as a prune. Sepp Dietrich looked like the muscular proprietor of a Marseilles bar. Martin Bormann was bent over like a retired bicycle champion. Apart from a few Nordic giants serving aperitifs on the terrace at Berchtesgaden, big, strong men with blond hair and cornflower-blue eyes did not abound in Hitler's entourage.

Imagine the surprise of the Germans descending through Russia, at meeting nothing but blue-eyed blondes. And such blondes! The exact type of the perfect Aryans that had been held up to them as ideals. Blond men and blond women.

Blondes everywhere: tall country girls, splendid and strong—with light-blue eyes—healthier and more vibrant than all Germany's assembled *Hitler-Jugend.* If one held to the sacrosanct canons of Hitlerism, one could not imagine a race more typically Aryan.

In six months, all the German armies had become Russophilic. They fraternized everywhere with the peasants. As under Napoleon, Europe was re-creating itself in the arms of the Europeans—especially these beautiful Russian girls, built for love and fertility, and who, during the retreat, were to be seen following bewilderedly, through the horror of the worst combat, their Erichs, Walters, Karls and Wolfgangs who had taught them, during off hours, that the pleasures of love have charms everywhere, even coming from the West.

Some Nazi theoreticians proclaimed violently anti-Slav theories. Even they could not have resisted 10 years of Russo-Germanic *rapprochement*. Russians of both sexes learned German very quickly. Often they already knew it. We found German textbooks in all the schools. The language barrier broke down more quickly in Russia than anywhere else in Europe.

The German possesses admirable qualities as a technician and organizer. But the Russian, a dreamer, is more imaginative and quick-witted. One completed the other. The attraction of the flesh would have done the rest. The young Germans, very naturally, and whatever their propaganda would have done to oppose it, would have married hundreds of thousands of young Russians.

They found them appealing. The creation of a united Europe in the east would have been completed in the most agreeable way. The Germano-Russian conjunction would have done wonders.

Yes, the problem was gigantic: to weld together 500 million Europeans, who had, in the beginning, no desire to coordinate their work, to combine their strengths, to harmonize their characters, their particular temperaments.

But Hitler carried in him the genius and the power capable of creating and imposing this gigantic oeuvre, on which hundreds of politicians had lost their footing—doomed by their mediocrity and the blinders they wore.

Hitler's millions of soldiers would have been there to back up his peace action, originating from all of Europe—the Europe of the Spanish *Division Azul* and of the Baltic warriors, of the Flanders Division and the Balkans Waffen-SS, of the *Division Charlemagne* from France and all the hundreds of thousands of German comrades in the 38 divisions of the Waffen-SS.

On our European promontory that juts off Asia into the western ocean, in what now remains of the West since the overthrow of the Third Reich, the first outposts have been built, after all—badly stocked and not yet very stable—of a Common Market eager to barter. All right. But a true Europe, uplifted by a heroic and revolutionary ideal, built on a grand scale, would have been something very different.[20]

The life of the youth of all Europe would have known a higher standard, and a better spirit than in leading an existence of roaming beatniks and protesters, justifiably in revolt against democratic regimes which never proposed any objective capable of inspiring them—repressing them, on the contrary—all through the mangy years of the postwar period.

The various European peoples would have been surprised to find in a German-led Europe that they ended up complementing each other so well. The popular plebiscites would have confirmed, to us still alive, that the Europe of compulsion had at last become, from the Pyrenees to the Urals, a united Free Europe, a community of 500 million Europeans in agreement.

It is a sad fact that in the 19th century Napoleon failed. His Europe, forged in the crucible of its epic history, would have saved us a lot of misfortunes—notably the two world wars. She would soon have taken the great world machine in her skilled hands, instead of letting Europe stew in the rivalries of colonialism, an abject and greedy project that in the end proved worthless.[21]

Similarly, it is unfortunate that in the 20th century Hitler failed. Communism would have been rejected. The United States would not have forced the world to bow to its dictatorship of ubiquitous military bases.

And, after 20 centuries of false starts and failed efforts, the sons of millions of Europeans, united in the beginning only in spite of themselves, would finally possess, together, the most powerful political, social, economic and intellectual consortium on the planet.

HITLERIAN EUROPE

"Would it have been a Europe of concentration camps?"

Are we going to have to listen to that same old tune forever? As if such camps have been built only in Europe. As if, after the downfall of Hitler, men had not continued to incarcerate or exterminate each other in Asia, in America, even in Europe, in the streets of Prague and Budapest.[22]

As if the invasions, the violations of territories, the abuses of power, the plots, the political kidnappings, had not flourished more than ever, in Vietnam, in Santo Domingo, in Venezuela, at the Bay of Pigs, even in the middle of Paris at the time of the Ben Barka affair, already forgotten. And even beyond the borders of Israel. Why not say it? For it is not Hitler, after all, who sped along with his tanks toward Mount Sinai and occupied by force the territories of others in the Near East.[23]

One must be—yes—against violence: that is, more precisely, against *all* violence—not only against the violence of Hitler, but also against the violence of Guy Mollet throwing thousands of paratroops on the Suez Canal in 1956, with as much premeditation as treachery.[24]

Perhaps one should also be against the violence of the Americans sniping, 17,000 miles away from Massachusetts or Florida, at the Vietnamese, whose lives they had no right to control. One should oppose the violence of the English, showering the Nigerians with weapons in order to free up oil wells for the super-capitalists, thanks to a million dead Biafrans.[25]

OPPOSE RED MURDERERS

One should be against the violence of the Soviet Union, flattening under their tanks the Hungarians and the Czechs who rejected their tyranny.

The same observation on the subject of war crimes:

Vanquished Germans were dragged to Nuremberg, locked up like monkeys in cages, and their defenders were forbidden to make use of any documents that might embarrass the accusers—notably all reference to the massacre in the Katyn Forest of 15,000 Polish officers—because the representative of Stalin, their murderer, was a member of the War Crimes Tribunal at Nuremberg instead of being indicted there.

If one claims the right to resort to such a procedure, let it be clearly understood that it must be for all criminals, not just for German criminals, but also for the British criminals who slaughtered 200,000 innocents in Dresden, for the French criminals who, without any legal procedure, shot defenseless German prisoners on their territory, and for the American criminals who crushed the sexual organs of SS prisoners from Malmedy and firebombed Tokyo.

War crime indictments were also merited by the Soviet criminals who ended World War II with horrifying cruelties in occupied Europe, and who crammed millions of people into their ghastly concentration camps in Siberia and the White Sea area.

However, those camps were not closed after World War II—as were those of the Third Reich, about which, 20 years after their "liberation," our ears were abused incessantly. [Similar camps in China still exist today, and still operate today. Thousands of human beings continue to be sent there who have had the misfortune to displease China's Communist rulers.—Ed.]

About those Communist camps, where the Reds implacably silence all those who oppose their dictatorship, none of the howlers of the left breathes a word. They wouldn't want any of their friends to be offended.[26]

Well then. Whence comes this concern about the truth? From fairness? Where is the good faith—and where is the fraud?

Who is the more repugnant, the one who kills or the virtuous ones who are silent as a mouse while the killing proceeds?

Observing the total impunity thus granted to criminals of war and peace as long as they are not German, all the postwar pirates have given themselves the pleasure of torturing victims to death with an atrocious savagery, *a la* Patrice Lumumba, finishing victims off with a machine pistol *a la* "Che" Guevara, assassinating prisoners in front of the press in the middle of Saigon with a revolver; setting up, with the complicity of the ultra-powerful, the public slaughter—like shooting toy ducks at a fair—of Kennedy I and then of Kennedy II, who were inconveniencing the real holders of power in the United States—the "intelligence" agencies and high finance, concealed beneath the bloody red cloak of democracy.[27]

HANG ALL CRIMINALS

All criminals to the dock: whoever they are, wherever they are.

Otherwise, all the virtuous, shrieking critics, indignant when it comes to acts of Hitler but silent when it is no longer about him, are abject con artists—converting the spirit of justice into their spirit of vengeance, and the censure of violence into the most tortuous hypocrisy.

Peace to the ashes of those who died under Hitler. But the hellish tom-tom beat, pounded incessantly on their urns by the false puritans of democracy, has become indecent. For more than 20 years this scandalous blackmail has continued throughout the world —scandalous because it is carried out with a bias as cynical as it is total.

One-way traffic is all right for narrow streets, but history is not so easily satisfied. She will not allow herself to be converted into a *cul-de-sac,* with the provokers of eternal hate stationed at the guard posts: they are whited sepulchers, full of dead men's bones; they are falsifiers; they are impostors.[28]

The result is the result. Despite the defeat in Russia, despite Hitler's body being burnt, and Benito Mussolini's body being hanged, the "fascisms" were, along with the advent of the Soviet system in Russia, the great events of the century. Some of the preoccupations of the Hitler of the 1930s have dimmed.

The notion of *Lebensraum* is old-fashioned. The proof: West Germany, reduced to a third the size of the original territory, is now richer and more powerful than the Hitlerian state of 1939.[29] Lower prices for international transportation over land and sea have changed everything. On a bare rock, strategically placed, one can now install the most powerful industries in the world.

The peasantry, so glorified by the "fascisms," has slipped down everywhere to the second rank. An intelligently industrialized farm brings in more now than 100 operations without economic rationalization and without precisely adapted modern equipment.

A majority previously, the peasants now form a smaller and smaller minority. Pasture and farm labor, expensive already in Sully's time, have ceased to be the sole source of nourishment of the peoples, all overfed or lacking enough money for food.[30]

GRAY MATTER RULES

And above all, the social doctrines, such as they were, that took account of only capital and labor, are obsolete.

A third element is intervening more and more: "gray matter." The economy is no longer a *ménage à deux*, but *à trois*. An ounce of creative intelligence is often more important than a trainload of coal or pyrites.

The brain has become the raw material *par excellence*. A scientific research laboratory can be worth more than an assembly line. Before the capitalist and before the worker: the researcher.

Without him, without his highly specialized facilities, without his computers and without his statistics, capital and labor are dead bodies. The Krupps themselves, and even the Rothschilds, have had to stand aside before the best brains.

The evolution of these problems did not catch Hitler off guard. He read everything and was informed of everything. His atomic laboratories were the best in the world. The essence of genius is to renew itself ceaselessly. Hitler, whose imagination was in continual combustion, would have continued to foresee the occurrences and the changes of our time. Above all, he was a molder of men.

Germany and Italy, although defeated and crushed (the Third Reich was no more than an enormous mound of bricks and debris in 1945), soon took the lead in early postwar Europe. Why? Because the great schools of Hitlerism and Fascism had built character. They had formed thousands of young leaders; had given a strong personality to thousands of human beings; it had revealed to them, in exceptional circumstances, their talents for organization and command that the silly, small, conventional routines of the previous times had never allowed them to display.

The German miracle after 1945 was this: a generation, physically crushed, had been exceptionally well-prepared for a leadership role by a doctrine based on authority, on responsibility and on a spirit of initiative; and by the baptism of fire.

It was found that this preparation had given their characters a temper of the best steel, which, at the time when they needed to get their country on its feet again, was revealed as an irresistible lever.

But Germany and Italy were not the only ones to be uplifted by the great Hitlerian hurricane. Our century was shaken by it down to the foundations, transformed in all fields, whether matters of state, social relations, the economy or scientific research.[31]

THE WORLD OF TODAY IS HITLER

The present spread of modern discoveries, from nuclear energy to miniaturization, is Hitler. Plug your ears if you like, but that's the way it is. Who got it under way, at a time when a somnolent Europe was eating her daily soup without caring to see any higher than the rim of the bowl?

What would a Wernher von Braun have become—a young, completely unknown Teuton without resources—if it had not been for Hitler? During his years of relative anonymity, the latter pushed him. Goebbels sometimes took over the shifts, supporting von Braun with his friendship. In 1944 again, this minister abandoned his other work in order to encourage von Braun personally.

It was the same story with hundreds of others. They had the talent. But what could they have done with only their own talent?

The Americans well knew that the scientific future of the world, in 1945, lay in Hitler's laboratories. Even though they now masquerade complacently as the kings of science and technical expertise, their biggest preoccupation, when they won the war in May 1945, was to hurry through the Third Reich, still smoking, to collect hundreds of scientists.

The Soviets were running a parallel race. They transported Hitlerian scholars to Moscow by the trainload.

To entice all those she was able to nab, America built golden bridges of opportunity. The U.S.A. chose as chief of their immense aerospace complex Hitler's von Braun, to whom modern America owes so much because it was he who first, in August 1939—even before World War II began—sent up the first of the world's rockets into the skies of Prussia. The modern world was born that day.

Just as gunpowder, which kills, also serves the world, the era opened by Hitler in 1939 will transform future centuries. In science as in the social domain, the denigrators of Hitler are merely his belated imitators. The Research Center of Pierrelate—is it anything but a copy of the Hitlerian base at Peenemuende—but 25 years late?[32]

Hitler has disappeared—and the democratic world has revealed itself incapable of creating anything new in the political and social domain, or even of patching up the old. It may try to prop back up on their skinny legs the battle-worn nags of the prewar period. Trembling, they fall back on the filthy ground.

From Gamal Nasser to de Gaulle, from Josip Tito to Fidel Castro, wherever one looks, among the old countries that seek a way out of the past or among the new countries of the Third World that are awakening—everywhere, the same formulas are resurgent: nationalism and socialism, and they are best represented by a strong man, the incarnation and the guide of the people, loving the power of the will, creating ideals and of faith.

The democratic myth of the old style, pompous, blathering, incompetent, sterile, is no more than a windbag with a hundred empty heads that does not fool anyone anymore or interest anyone anymore, and makes the young laugh in scorn.

NEVER TO BE FORGOTTEN

Who worries anymore about the old prewar parties and their devalued and forgotten big shots? Ah, but Hitler and Mussolini—who will ever forget them? Millions of our boys died at the end of a horrible odyssey. What has become of even their poor tombs, over there, so far away? Our lives, those of the survivors, have been crushed, pillaged, eliminated for good. But the fascisms, for which we lived, have shaped our epoch forever. In the midst of our misfortunes that is our great joy.

It's no use to scrape the SS tattoos off from the arms of our soldiers. Too late. We gaze at the exterminators and defy them.

The curtain of history has fallen over Hitler and Mussolini, as it fell over Napoleon. The dwarves will be able to change nothing. The Great Revolution of the 20th century has been accomplished. ✦

ENDNOTES:

1 As historian David Irving pointed out in his two-volume *Churchill's War,* the arch-imperialist Churchill destroyed his own beloved empire. Among other things, he bankrupted it both economically and morally. Why should black Africans or brown Indians respect any longer the white masters who had twice (in WWI and WWII) slaughtered one another like wild animals? There was no more white moral superiority after 1945, only a technological advantage.

2 Churchill had vowed publicly that the British empire would indeed fight on from Canada and other outposts of its empire. Until 1947, Canadian passports listed the bearer as a "British subject."

In his well-written "We Shall Fight on the Beaches" speech of June 4, 1940, to the House of Commons, he implied that Canada and the United States would save England: "We shall fight on the beaches, we shall fight on the landing grounds, we shall fight in the fields and in the streets, we shall fight in the hills; we shall never surrender, and even if, which I do not for a moment believe, this island or a large part of it were subjugated and starving, then our empire beyond the seas, armed and guarded by the British Fleet, would carry on the struggle, until, in God's good time, the New World, with all its power and might, steps forth to the rescue and the liberation of the old."

3 The count of Saint-Simon (1760-1825) founded socialism, the doctrine that the state should directly run and own the economy, decades before Karl Marx. Highly eccentric and dying in direst poverty, the French nobleman's ideas nevertheless lived on in many new forms. One key idea was that philosophy divides men into warring egos whereas real religion unites, and it saves the poor, who were the focus of his concerns. His later fellow blue-blood Charles de Gaulle was extremely anti-Communist and did all he could in his long presidency (1958-1969) of France to improve the lot of workers, partly so they would not vote for the huge French Communist Party, which was subsidized by Moscow. See TBR January/February 2008.

4 Churchill was ecstatic at the news of Pearl Harbor, the *"deus ex machina"* that brought the U.S. into the war, writing later in *The Second World War* of his feelings: "So we had won after all. . . . Hitler's fate was sealed. . . . I went to bed and slept the sleep of the saved and thankful." Degrelle consistently reserved his most corrosive invective, of which he was a past master, for Winston Churchill, whom he considered a monstrous creature—and the destroyer of Degrelle's own vision and career. In the TBR DVD *Hitler's Blitzkrieg II,* one can see and hear Degrelle pronouncing *"ce Churchill"* ("this Churchill") with loathing: "Suh Shur-SHEEL."

5 Hugh Capet was crowned king of the Western Franks in 987.

6 When these memoirs were published in 1969, "holocaust" Revisionism had still made no impact on the public or even on many white nationalists. Leon Degrelle became a sharp foe of the gas chambers stories later in life.

In any case, in the Waffen-SS he had no contact with concentration camps, ruled by the "Regular (or 'General') SS," and in fact was never accused of any atrocities against Jews on the eastern front. He was condemned to death *in absentia* in Belgium for "treason."

7 Saint Bartholomew's Day on August 24, 1572, was one of the bloodiest days for Europe's Christians, staining the history of France forever. More than 425 years later, Saint Bartholomew's Day is still remembered with horror. The murders of French Protestants, or Huguenots, began in Paris with the slaughter of 3,000 wedding celebrants. In all of France, 70,000 Protestants were killed.

8 It was a common practice in many white, Western countries until recently to offer alcohol—whiskey, wine, beer or vodka—at political meetings or even on Election Day to enhance the electorate's sober judgment.

9 Regional differences in the United States, a country tied together quickly by trains, telegraph, telephones, televisions, jets and the Internet, are far less divisive than in Europe. Even in tiny Austria, the size of Maine, different sections of even the selfsame valley mock each other. In the Upper Inn River Valley west of Innsbruck, the locals claim: "If an Upper Inn girl gives you a kiss, a Lower Inn girl would give you an illegitimate child." One Viennese who had lived for 25 years in the mountainous Tyrol told the translator: "I know that if I live here another 25 years, I will never be accepted by these Tyroleans."

In the same way, northern and southern Germans have long disliked each other. Northern Englishmen despise Londoners as effeminate and snobbish, and the Londoners view northerners as uncouth barbarians. A Ukrainian informed us that Russian-speaking Ukrainians were "too stupid to know anything," while a Russian revealed that "Ukrainians can never be trusted." This is universal. The inhabitants of Tokyo, Japan view those of Osaka as embarrassingly loud money-grubbers whose greeting is "Making money?"; the Osakans see Tokyoites as stuffed-shirt weirdos who eat rotten soybeans.

10 Hitler's agriculture minister, who popularized the slogan "Blood and Soil," was Walther von Darré (1895-1953), of French Huguenot descent. He wrote the famous 1928 book *Das Bauerntum als Lebensquell der nordischen Rasse* ["Farm families as the fountain of life of the Nordic race"]. Conversely, hundreds of thousands of German settlers had spread out, over several centuries, across the Baltic countries, in Hungary, in Romania, and even 150,000 along the Volga. The Flemish, who moved down in significant numbers into the north of France, gave to this region its most tenacious industrial elite. The benefits of these cohabitations were just as noticeable in the Latin areas. The Spaniards of the left, who had no choice but to take refuge in France after their debacle of 1939, are themselves, in one generation, mistaken for the French who welcomed them: Maria Casarès, daughter of the prime minister of the Frente Popular, became one of the most admired actresses at the Theatre Français. Hundreds of thousands of Italians were pushed into France by hunger during the last century—they too assimilated extremely easily. To such a degree that one of the greatest writers of France of the last century was the son of a Venetian: Emile Zola. In our time, French writers of Italian ancestry are legion, Jean Giono at their head.

11 Today's European Union, for all its pernicious secret agenda of race-mixing Arabs, Turks and Africans with white Europeans, has succeeded in mixing different white European stocks as well. Millions of Europeans now live, work and intermarry in one anothers' countries, often using English as a neutral tongue to communicate.

12 Between WWI and WWII, Austria saw fierce violence between left and right. After WWII, this did not repeat itself; the various leaders had all had to get along from 1938-45 in German concentration camps.

13 Leon Degrelle, after retiring from his successful construction company—which discreetly helped build some U.S. air bases in Spain—lived in Màlaga, on the Mediterranean Costa del Sol.

14 While both symbols are less militaristic today, both are alive and well in 2007. One Frenchman stated to this translator: "The *coq* [=rooster] is the true symbol of the Frenchman. He is macho, makes hens happy, and he still sings even when standing up to his knees in chicken manure." At the 2006 World Cup in Germany, millions of young Germans, for the first time since the war, were flying their flag (now a black-red-gold tricolor) with a fierce black German eagle with red claws and beak on the front.

15 The European Union, by 2008, has begun to achieve the material prosperity that Europe could have had 50 years earlier, following a German victory. Economies are finally booming in Mediterranean, Baltic and Slavic areas that have not been prosperous for centuries. Of course, much of this boom has come from borrowed money and it

is being half-consumed by the staggering social costs of immigration into Europe by Turks, Arabs and Africans. In general, however, an economically united Europe—with the German economy at the center—has become very wealthy, in some ways wealthier than the U.S., just as Degrelle foresaw in 1969.

16 Just as Great Britain was England, Cornwall, Wales, Scotland, the Isle of Man and Northern Ireland, Greater Germany, *Grossdeutschland,* was the union of Germany proper, Austria, Sudetenland, Alsace (in France) and, some predicted for the future, Holland, Flanders (in Belgium) and the Germanic parts of Switzerland, all areas that were lost by Germany in 1648 and where, in a scientific, linguistic sense, German dialects are spoken. Germans and the Dutch can read 85% of each other's newspapers with ease.

17 France had bought the island of Corsica from Genoa in 1768, the year before Napoleon's birth to a family of minor nobility; the Corsicans, speaking an Italian dialect similar to Tuscan and living off the coast of Italy itself, were neither consulted nor happy, and some to this day still are angry about it; bombs still explode, and a French prefect was assassinated in 1998. The Corsicans speak Corsu, or Lingua Corsa, a Latin derivative, and Napoleon never lost his Italianate Corsican accent when he spoke French.

18 The description of all things German as "heavy" is a universal Latin viewpoint, denoting both robust and strong on the one hand—Latins thus buy many German cars—and humorless and rigid on the other. It is instructive to visit Strasbourg, which has had long periods of both German and French rule. On the campus of the university of Strasbourg, one can instantly tell which buildings were erected under the Kaisers—the massive ones, almost nuclear blast-proof, and which were French—the ones that seem to dance. Crossing the Rhine is like a trip between two different fields of energy, between yin and yang.

19 Hitler could probably be characterized as a member of the Alpine subrace of whites, rather than the Nordic subrace. He had the brachycephalic head shape of the Alpines and Dinarics.

20 The six-member European Economic Community, often called "the Common Market," was founded in 1957. French President Charles de Gaulle, by his veto, kept Britain out of it during his long tenure, 1958-69, once quipping that Britain, since 1941, has been "the aircraft carrier of the United States."

The Common Market's *de facto* successor as of 1992, under the Maastricht Treaty, is the European Union (which now has 27 member states, Macedonia having joined in 2004), 500 million inhabitants and, as of 2006, had an $11 trillion economy with still very important factory production, unlike the United States, which has become a "service economy."

The administrative capital is, ironically, the main city of Leon Degrelle's youth, Brussels, Belgium. The European Parliament, which is elected by proportional voting and thus must admit a "Heritage Bloc" representing the white nationalists, is located in a gleaming glass building in Strasbourg, Alsace, near the French-German border—representing the union of Germanic and Latin Europe that Degrelle lived for. There can be no doubt that if white nationalists came to power across Europe, they would not scrap the European Union *per se*, but likely rename it and instantly change its policies of non-white immigration and political correctness. But the vision Hitler and Degrelle had of a United Europe, albeit right now in the wrong hands, is coming to fruition; Europe is slowly moving toward superpower status.

21 Charles de Gaulle revealed to his confidant and adviser Alain Peyrefitte that he had decided to end France's colonial empire in Africa because (1) the Arab/Berber and black colonies cost France more than they produced, especially through guerrilla movements that had to be suppressed, and (2) to prevent those Africans from moving to France. But five years after his death, Valery Giscard d'Estaing, a supposed Gaullist with strong ties to the Grand Orient of French Freemasonry, pushed through a new immigration law of "family reunification," which, as in the United States, allowed every non-white to bring in his relatives. Thus France, like England, Holland and Belgium, got rid of its colonies but then brought its colonials into white Europe—thus getting the worst of both worlds.

22 Degrelle is referring to the 1968 Czech and 1956 Hungarian uprisings against the Soviets. Most westerners, including even Degrelle, then underground and in Spanish exile, ignore the East German uprising of June 17, 1953, which the Soviets also crushed with tanks. The USSR declared martial law in 90% of "East Germany," which was covered with strikes and the storming of Communist prisons to liberate political prisoners.

Presumably, Germans can never be depicted or even imagined as freedom fighters rising in revolt. (Lenin once joked that Germans would never storm any government building as long as there were little signs on the front lawn: "*Verboten* to walk on the grass.")

Nevertheless, June 17 became an important holiday in West Germany, "German Unity Day," until Germany was reunited in 1990-91. It is still called National Memorial Day for the 55 "East Germans" killed.

23 Mehdi Ben Barka (1920-65) was a left-wing Moroccan politician who traveled the world supporting Castro, "Che" Guevara, an end to apartheid in South Africa and the overthrow of Morocco's king, Hassan II. On a trip to Paris on October 29, 1965, he disappeared. *Time* magazine in 1975 suggested blame fell on the Mossad, the French secret police, the Moroccan king and also the CIA, which refused to release 1,800 pages on the disappearance despite the Freedom of Information Act. Supposedly a CIA agent known as "Col. Martin" showed the Moroccans how to dissolve his cadaver in a vat of acid in an act of "professional courtesy," while his head went to the king. In any case, this democracy-approved murder was one of the causes célèbres of the 1960s.

24 Mollet (1905-75) was a Socialist Party activist who, as prime minister of France in 1956-57, landed French paratroops in Egypt to take back the Suez Canal, which French stockholders co-owned with Britain, from Col. Gamal Abdel Nasser, the charismatic Arab nationalist who then led Egypt. Two-thirds of Europe's oil came through the Suez Canal. Britain and Israel also attacked Egypt; President Dwight Eisenhower, despite his promises to his NATO allies in London and Paris, opposed all three countries at the UN and forced them to make a humiliating withdrawal. (Eisenhower threatened to dump U.S. holdings of the British pound sterling to cause its collapse, and to not sell any oil to Britain, then facing an oil crisis since Nasser sank all 40 ships then in the canal, blocking it for months.)

The British suddenly withdrew their troops without pre-notifying the French, whose forces were fighting in Cairo; Charles de Gaulle, then preparing to return to power, decided that the United States not only controlled Britain but that neither were reliable allies if it came to war.

Mollet also ordered a "surge" of French troops into Arabic-speaking Algeria to put down the Algerian revolt against French rule. The Battle of Algiers (Jan.-Oct. 1957) was the result. The French, through both ruthless combat and torture, crushed the insurrection in the Algerian capital, although this did not end the war.

To this day, "molletism" in France is a scathing leftist word meaning a liberal-talking politician who does "right-wing" things.

25 The Biafran War of 1967-70 saw mostly Christian Biafrans (predominantly of the Ibo or Igbo tribe) in the south of Nigeria try to break away from the more Muslim north; aided by Britain and the USSR, the Nigerian central government won and Britain's friends kept its oil interests. Nigeria today lives exclusively off oil, aside from "the 419 scam," where Americans learn by ungrammatical emails from Nigeria that, without entering it, they have won the British National Lottery and should send their bank account information to Nigerians. (Biafra, it is said, existed as an empire several thousand years before Nigeria was cobbled together by a British governor, Sir Frederick Luggard, for the convenience of Western bankers.)

26 A disgraceful Wikipedia article on the subject "Gulag" engages in a "limited hang-out": yes, conditions were tough, yes—but not tough enough to list even one time one number to show how many millions died there. (Presumably 17 to 22 million died in the gulag.) The obscene apologia ends by reasoning from *The Moscow Times*, partner of *The New York Times* and *Wall Street Journal* and owned by the Finnish Jewish press baron Aatos Erkko.

The big question was why there were no "post-Communism trials" for the organizers and wardens of the gulag, which may have actually killed close to 30 million white Christians. Answer: "The gulag had already killed tens of thousands of its own most ardent killers. Again and again, yesterday's judges were declared today's criminals, so that Soviet society never had to own up to its millions of state-backed murders." So all Stalin's executioners themselves died conveniently in the gulag. This explains why the Jewish mastermind of the gulag and the starvation genocide of the Ukrainians, "Iron Lazar" Moisevich Kaganovich, died in his cushy Moscow apartment in 1991 at age 97.

27 Patrice Lumumba (1925-1961) was the first democratically elected prime minister of the Democratic Republic of the Congo after its independence from Belgium. With the aid of the future tyrant Joseph Mobutu—one of Africa's worst, and who renamed the country Zaire—and of Mobutu's allies in the CIA and the Belgian military, he was deposed as a Communist sympathizer after two months, beaten numerous times, including on television,

by Congolese soldiers and was then shot by Belgian officers. A Belgian officer then dissolved his skull with acid and showed some of his teeth to the press. The Belgian government in 2002 admitted its responsibility.

Ernesto Guevara de la Serna, an Argentine aristocrat of part-Irish ancestry who became a medical doctor, then revolutionary soldier under the name "Che," went to Bolivia from Cuba in 1967 to stir up a popular socialist revolution, was wounded and captured. The prisoner was then shot at the urging of the CIA. His body was displayed, thrown in a bathtub, to the world media, and his hands ghoulishly cut off. His wristwatch and personal effects are now displayed at CIA headquarters. He was buried under a runway; but his remains now reside in honor in Cuba.

The famous Alex Korda photo of him, seen on t-shirts worldwide and considered the most widely viewed image of the 20th century, was taken at the 1960 funeral of 100 dock workers killed in a suspicious explosion in Havana harbor. Guevara, as an M.D., had tended to many of the wounded and dying.

John Kennedy, who wished to prevent Israel from obtaining atomic weapons, was publicly killed in 1963; his brother Robert, a skilled legal investigator and major presidential candidate, was assassinated in 1968; and John Kennedy Jr., who had become a journalist, perished in 1999; the U.S. government ruled it was not homicide.

28 Degrelle, a Christian, is referring to Jesus's words denouncing the Sanhedrin: "Alas for you, ye scribes and Pharisees, hypocrites, for you are just like whitewashed sepulchers, the outside of which pleases the eye, though inside they are full of dead men's bones and of all that is unclean." (Matthew 23:27)

29 In fact, according to Joaquin Bochaca, in his book *The Crimes of the "Good Guys"* (see excerpt in the May/June 2007 TBR, pp. 36-37), Hitler's approach, during the 1930s, to the problem of *Lebensraum* for the German people—his *Drang nach Osten*—was not a program of military conquest, but an economic-political plan similar in many ways to today's European Union. Of course, by the time Degrelle became well acquainted with the Fuehrer personally, World War II had intervened, and the military conquest of all the countries concerned was a *fait accompli.*

30 Maximilien de Béthune, duke of Sully (1560-1641), was the great soldier, government minister, staunch Protestant, developer of the French military and of French agriculture for his master, Henry IV of France.

31To demand excellence and the highest achievement from every farmer, worker, soldier, party activist, artist and schoolgirl was an innovation of the Third Reich, and resulted in the phenomena of both the expanding Third Reich and of the booming, swiftly recovering postwar West Germany.

32 France under Charles de Gaulle, using the nuclear research center at Pierrelate, became the country with the highest percentage in the world of its electricity from nuclear power, making the country far less vulnerable to oil cutoffs. The [German] Army Research Center at Peenemuende, on an small German island in the Baltic, was started in 1937 and run by Wernher von Braun. It developed Germany's V-1 and V-2 rockets.

BELGIAN WAFFEN SS GEN. LEON DEGRELLE fought not only for his country but for the survival of Christian Europe, preventing the continent from being inundated by Stalin's savage hordes. What Degrelle has to say, as an eyewitness to some of the key events in the history of the 20th century, is vastly important within the historical and factual context of his time and has great relevance to the continuing struggle today for the survival of civilization as we know it. Gen. Degrelle was translated by ***JOHN NUGENT***, a former Marine translator, linguist, European-American rights activist and public office seeker.

NOTE: This article first appeared in the March/April 2008 issue of the bimonthly historical journal THE BARNES REVIEW. TBR is $46 for one year. Call 1-877-773-9077 toll free to order or visit www.barnesreview.com.

John Amery: British Traitor?

A New Revisionist Look at a Controversial Character

FOR SURE, MOST AMERICANS HAVE NEVER HEARD OF JOHN AMERY, the Briton who defected from his mother country before World War II. But here is populist publisher Willis A. Carto's brief account of an anti-Communist hero blackballed by history.

BY WILLIS A. CARTO

In broadcasts to his homeland, Britain, before and during World War II, John Amery cogently argued his reasons for supporting Germany and her allies, making it very clear that England's declaration of war on Germany on Sept. 3, 1939, was a ghastly mistake, a mistake which could result only in England's loss of her empire, national bankruptcy, American domination and loss of British sovereignty. Of course, that's exactly what happened.

Few are the observers who, before WWII, described the incipient war as "this hopeless, lunatic war in which we are losers, whatever happens."

In the book, Amery attacks Churchill as a duplicitous traitor who knowingly sold out his country's future to Zionist interests after accepting a loan of 150,000 pounds from a Jewish leader. In retrospect, this incident is the most weighty in Churchill's political life, so we will quote Amery's entire passage:

> Readers curious about the reasons for Churchill's strange change of position may like to consider that, by 1938, when he was 64, Churchill had so lived beyond his means that his creditors prepared to foreclose on him. He was faced with the prospect of the forced sale of his luxurious country estate,

John Amery (1912-1945) was a British citizen, part Jewish, who proposed to Adolf Hitler the forming of a British and Dominion anti-Communist volunteer force (which subsequently became the British Free Corps). He made recruitment efforts and propaganda broadcasts for Nazi Germany and was executed for treason after the war. Here, Amery is arrested by police in the Salò Republic (Repubblica Sociale Italiana). He was sent to Wandsworth Prison in England to be hanged. Amery's wife, Una, is shown at left escorted by two more police officers.

Chartwell. At this hour of crisis a dark and mysterious figure entered Churchill's life: Henry Strakosch, a multi-millionaire Jew who had acquired a fortune speculating in South African mining ventures. . . . Strakosch stepped forward, advanced the ageing demagogue a "loan" of 150,000 pounds just in time to save his estate from the auctioneer, then quietly slipped into the background again. In the years that followed, Strakosch served as Churchill's adviser and confidant but miraculously managed to avoid the spotlight. . . .

Amery rather clearly proves the point by quoting Churchill both before and after his acceptance of the loan, showing the incredible, criminal hypocrisy of this pompous humbug who at first supported Prime Minister Neville Chamberlain and his peace policy, then abruptly turned pro-war after the loan.

England, then the world's preeminent sea power, and Germany, dominating the European continent, were natural allies to confront the atheistic, murderous regime of Josef Stalin, argues Amery, citing the figures available then of Bolshevik Russia's willing (and mostly Jewish) executioners, not remotely comparable to the Nazi toll.

After the war, Amery was tried for treason in England and hanged, closing his mouth forever.

A close look at the words of John Amery (available on the Internet) will quickly counter those establishment historians—addicted to journalistic propaganda passing as history—who smear Amery as a traitor. ✦

WILLIS A. CARTO is the publisher of TBR. He has also published hundreds of books of interest to Nationalists and patriots. He was the founder of LIBERTY LOBBY (1955)and the publisher of *The Spotlight* newspaper from 1975 to 2001. Currently he is the publisher of AMERICAN FREE PRESS newspaper (1-888-699-NEWS).

NOTE: This article first appeared in the January/February 2008 issue of the bimonthly historical journal THE BARNES REVIEW (www.barnesreview.org).

THE DISCLAIMER AIRED DURING JOHN AMERY'S RADIO BROADCASTS

"Tonight you will here an Englishman who is speaking to you at his own request and of his own free will: Mr. John Amery, son of Secretary for India of the British government, the Rt. Honorable Leopold Stennett Amery. The German government bears no responsibility whatever for what Mr. Amery is going to say. The German government has merely thought fit to place its station at the disposal of Mr. Amery for what he desires to say. We believe that Mr. Amery's observations will be of special interest to you also."

In the maverick tradition of one of the great historians of the modern era . . .

No topic is "too controversial" for THE BARNES REVIEW, the most interesting history magazine published anywhere today. Commemorating the trailblazing path of the towering 20th century revisionist historian, the late Harry Elmer Barnes, TBR's mission is to separate historical truth from propaganda and to bring history into accord with the facts. Founded in 1994 by veteran American nationalist Willis A. Carto—a personal friend of Barnes—THE BARNES REVIEW concurs with Rousseau's maxim "falsification of history has done more to impede human development than any one thing known to mankind." TBR covers all aspects of history from the dawn of man to recent events and also places a special focus on the philosophy of nationalism. As such, TBR proudly describes itself as a "journal of nationalist thought" and dares to be politically incorrect in a day when Cultural Marxism prevails in the mass media, in academia and in day-to-day life. TBR's editorial board of advisors encompasses historians, philosophers and academics from all over the face of the planet, intellectuals united in their desire to bring peace to the world by exposing the lies and prevarications of the past that have brought us to where we are today. If you believe everything you see in the "responsible" media or think that absolutely everything that appears in most college-level history texts is true, you might be shocked by what you see in TBR—but if you are shocked by what you see in TBR, then that's all the more reason you need to join the growing ranks of independent-minded thinkers from all walks of life and all over the world who are longtime TBR subscribers.

Isn't it time you subscribe?

The Barnes Review $46 for ONE year (six bimonthly issues—64 pages each); Including this special free bonus: A FREE COPY OF Michael Collins Piper's blockbuster book *Share the Wealth: Huey Long vs Wall Street.* That's a $20 gift free for a one-year domestic subscription. Subscribe for two years at $78 and get *Share the Wealth* PLUS *A Short History of the Balfour Declaration.* Outside the U.S. email sales@barnesreview.com for international rates and for S&H to your nation.

Call 1-877-773-9077 today and charge a subscription to major credit cards or send your check, money order or credit card information (including expiration date) to:

THE BARNES REVIEW, P.O. Box 15877, Washington, D.C. 20003

Check us out at www.barnesreview.com

CPSIA information can be obtained at www.ICGtesting.com
Printed in the USA
BVOW05s2342130815

413154BV00001B/1/P